Walhachin —
Catastrophe or Camelot?

Joan Weir

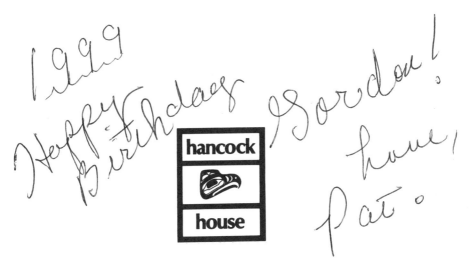

1999 Happy Birthday Gordon! love, Pat.

hancock house

Work crew camp at Walhachin during preparatory work on the orchard lands.

The story of Walhachin says something
of the unconquerable spirit of man.
That spirit has shaped our past
and will surely guarantee our future.
And to that spirit
this book is respectfully dedicated.

ISBN 0-88839-982-0

Second Printing 1995

Production and layout by Dorothy Forbes

Printed in Canada

Published simultaneously in Canada and the United States by

HANCOCK HOUSE PUBLISHERS LTD.
19313 Zero Avenue, Surrey, B.C. V4P 1M7
(604) 538-1114   Fax (604) 538-2262

HANCOCK HOUSE PUBLISHERS
1431 Harrison Avenue, Blaine, WA 98230-5005
(604) 538-1114   Fax (604) 538-2262

Table of Contents

Acknowledgements

I am indebted to Nelson A. Riis, MP, for permission to use the factual material contained in his unpublished Master's thesis entitled "Settlement Abandonment," which he submitted to the Department of Geography at the University of British Columbia in 1970.

I am also indebted to Ida Makaro, editor of the Ashcroft Journal, for permission to research the Ashcroft Journal files from 1909 to 1922, and to Ross Phelps, editor of the Kamloops Sentinel, for permission to research the Inland Sentinel files from 1909 to 1919; to the curator and the staff at the Kamloops Museum; to the staff at the Provincial Archives in Victoria; to Anna Selme in Walhachin; to Peggy Gilmour and Gordon Parke for photographs and letters from family albums; and to all those individuals who assisted with personal information about the orchard settlement.

Joan Weir

Picking the fall apple crop.

The Great Idea

The Thompson River valley, showing the benchlands high above the level of the water. Early buidings (1910) of townsite visible.

The orchard settlement at Walhachin has been described in many controversial terms. Some people have called the clearing of sagebrush and cactus from 5,000 acres (2,024 hectares) of desert fields and the planting of hundreds of thousands of apple trees, a romantic adventure. Perhaps it was.

Others have termed this settlement of Englishmen with their formal dress and their Mayfair manners in the isolation of the British Columbia wilderness, a Canadian Camelot. And perhaps it was this, too. Certainly, no one can deny that Walhachin had its "brief shining moment" during the nine years that it prospered.

The residents of the neighboring towns branded these titled upper-class Englishmen, who were convinced of their superiority by reason of the simple fact that they were English, as being "class-conscious" and "snobbish." Undoubtedly, they were both of these things. In addition, they were singularly ill-equipped for either frontier living or for fruit farming, having no practical skills of any kind. They were also stubborn, insular and narrow-minded, with the result that they brought a great many of their problems on themselves.

But nevertheless, it is hard to be too critical, because in many instances they were misled — the recipients of inaccurate information. It is also impossible to avoid admiring them in spite of their bulldog stubbornness and their inbred prejudice, for they were resourceful, determined and courageous. In fact, unless one is careful, one may even find himself envying them a little. For having found themselves committed to an impossible undertaking, this mixed assortment of gentlemen orchardists united only by their love of England, their fondness for leisured upper-class living and their singular lack of any training or expertise which might have helped them with the project at hand, came very close to succeeding in turning the desert into a garden.

It began in 1907 in the mind of Charles E. Barnes, an American, who at that time was working as a land surveyor out of Ashcroft, British Columbia.

Barnes was a strong, good-looking man, able and intelligent. He was immensely likeable and a natural leader, probably because of his boundless energy and enthusiasm. He was a man of great determination, whose vocabulary contained no such phrase as "too difficult." He was also an entrepreneur.

Shortly after his arrival in Ashcroft he had visited the ranch of Charles Pennie, which was situated on the south shore of the Thompson River some fifteen miles (24 kilometres) east of where Barnes was working. He had been impressed by the two-acre apple orchard which flourished next to the Pennie ranch house, and in the weeks that followed this visit, the possibility of developing the whole valley into an orchard caught his imagination.

The mood of the time gave this vision substance. All across Canada people were talking "orchards." In British Columbia, the feeling was particularly strong that fruit growing was equally as lucrative, and a great deal less risky, than heading to Barkerville or searching the Klondike for gold as so many Canadians had done just a decade before. Consequently, when Barnes casually mentioned his idea to a number of his associates, he met with no discouragement.

It is unfortunate that Barnes had so recently arrived in British Columbia or he would have realized that the existence of a two-acre orchard on the Pennie ranch was no indication of the growing capacity of the entire property. It was customary for farmers and for ranchers in western Canada to plant a small orchard in order to provide their families with much-needed fruit during the long Canadian winters. However, the site of this orchard was chosen with great care. The trees were planted on the most arable bit of land available close to a ready source of irrigation and, invariably, where they would have some protection from the winter winds. If Barnes had looked more closely at the entire Pennie property he would have realized that Pennie's orchard had been planted on the only two-acre piece of land that could possibly have supported it. It was the only area free of rocks — it alone lay adjacent to one of the few creeks in the whole area — and it alone possessed a natural windbreak provided by the surrounding higher ground which protected the fruit trees from the killing winds which blew all winter off the Thompson River. Barnes, however, through, inexperience, assumed that the whole ranch property would prove equally arable, and encouraged by the healthy appearance of Pennie's fruit trees, set about to realize his orchard dream.

His first move was to find the necessary financial backing for his project; his second, to attract the type of settler he felt could make a success of the project. And for this he looked to England to a company called the British Columbia Development Association, which had been founded in 1895.

This company had already demonstrated a willingness to invest in development projects in British Columbia. They were the financial backers of the 2,000-acre 111-Mile House Ranch and Hotel on the Cariboo Road, and of the Nicola Land Company Limited (Beaver Ranch). In addition, they held shares in the Alaska and North West Trading Company and in the North Pacific Wharves and Trading Company.[1] Moreover, they seemed determined to attract the kind of colonist that Barnes wanted. Their Memorandum of Association defined the aims of the British Columbia Development Association (BCDA) as being:

"1. To develop the resources of British Columbia, and therein to promote commercial and financial enterprise.

"2. To promote, organize and conduct the colonization of British Columbia by the introduction of suitable emigrants from Great Britain.

"3. Generally, to develop property and estates for the company by promoting immigration, selling (and) leasing and by establishing villages and settlements.

"4. To carry on . . . the business of farmers, graziers, meat and fruit preservers, brewers . . . and any other businesses which may seem calculated to develop the company's property or to benefit its interests."[2]

It seemed to Barnes that the BCDA would be the perfect

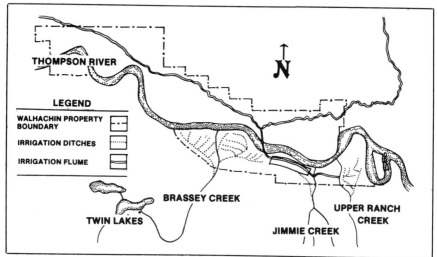

backers for his orchard settlement. Accordingly, he invited Sir William Bass, one of the leading directors of the BCDA, together with a qualified agriculturalist and a trained engineer to come out to view the Thompson River valley to assess its potential as an orchard area.

It should be noted here that neither the agriculturalist nor the engineer whom Barnes invited was likely to have reached a decision as to the suitability of the Pennie ranch for orchard development without at least a trace of bias, because both men were employed on the English estate of Lord Aberdeen, and John Campbell Gordon, 7th Earl of Aberdeen, was an orchard enthusiast. In 1891 Gordon had purchased a large tract of land near Vernon, British Columbia, for the purpose of establishing an orchard of his own, and this orchard had been entirely successful. Whether or not this fact might have influenced Messrs. Palmer and Ashcroft to look more favorably on Barnes' scheme than they might otherwise have done is open to conjecture, but in any case, whether it was the result of wishful thinking or of considered judgement, the two men seemingly paid no attention whatever to the sandy nature of the soil, the preponderance of rocks, the absence of any adequate source of water for irrigation or to the climate conditions. They endorsed Barnes' plan without reservation. And Sir William Bass, acting on this endorsement, recommended to the London-based BCDA that it should borrow the necessary capital to purchase the site of the Pennie ranch and to proceed with the development of an orchard settlement on the banks of the Thompson River in British Columbia.

Accordingly, on January 21, 1908, C.H. Wilkinson, the managing director of the BCDA in London and E.E. Billinghurst, the provincial manager of the BCDA in Victoria, bought the Pennie ranch. They also bought the adjacent 930 acres which J.B. Greaves had previously owned. The price paid, according to the Ashcroft Journal of January, 1908, was $200 per acre which amounted to a total purchase price of $229,400 for the land, the existing buildings, the livestock and a certain amount of additional leased land.

The BCDA then transferred Sir Talbot Chetwynd, the cattle manager of their 111-Mile House Ranch, to the Pennie ranch with instructions to dispose of all the cattle which had belonged to the previous owner, and to begin the transformation of grazing land into orchard fields. The BCDA then created two companies: The British Columbia Horticultural Estates Limited, which would deal with the agricultural development, and the Dry Belt Settlement Utilities Limited, which would oversee the development of the townsite.

Until this time the name of the train station at the site of the ranch had been Pennie's, but now the BCDA chose a new name for its orchard settlement. It was Walhassen, an Indian name, which the company euphemistically translated as meaning "bountiful valley," though the Indians themselves insisted, according to former Kamloops Museum curator Mary Balf's research,[3] that the meaning was closer to "land of round rocks." Whether it was because of this disagreement or because of some other reason, in 1909 the name was changed to Walhachin (pronounced Walla-sheen) which the company later defined in its brochure as "an Indian word signifying an abundance of food products of the earth." Meantime, Charles Barnes had been established as manager of the B.C. Horticultural Estates Company. He purchased an additional 3,265 acres of land on the north bank of the Thompson River from the Dominion government for a nominal fee of one dollar per acre on the understanding that the British Columbia Horticultural Estates Company would provide water for its total development. This new acreage lay directly opposite the Pennie and Greaves ranches.

Now the business of promoting the orchard enterprise moved rapidly ahead. Representatives of the BCDA in London carried out the initial advertising campaign through word of mouth promotion; later an attractive thirty-page brochure was printed. From the beginning, the promotion met with remarkable success. Most purchasers bought their ten-acre

11

holdings without showing the slightest concern at not being able to view their newly-acquired property in advance. Perhaps the main reason for this success was that the promoters had recognized the importance of presenting a vision of a complete lifestyle. It was not only the financial opportunities which were being extolled, but a whole leisured, fashionable and satisfying way of life was being offered to the would-be investor.

In keeping with the avowed intention of the BCDA to attract only "suitable emigrants" to its various projects, it was made fairly clear that only upper-class Englishmen would be encouraged to buy a share in this stylish orchard settlement. It was also made clear that life at Walhachin would be leisured and comfortable, that the climate would be ideal, that social niceties would prevail and that sports activities would be varied and numerous. The promise was made that a monorail would be constructed to link all parts of the settlement. Potential orchardists were also assured that their investment would realize an immediate profit. They were told that their ten-acre holdings could be depended upon to yield six-hundred pounds of apples annually and that until their fruit trees had reached maturity, they would be assured of a steady income from the intermediate vegetable crops which could be planted between the rows of seedling trees, which would yield more than four-hundred pounds of marketable produce every fall.[4]

The advertising even described a horticultural school that the company intended to establish which would instruct the new orchardists in the best possible methods of fruit growing and orchard management.

Undeniably, this advertising was more romantic than factual — certainly no horticultural school ever materialized, nor did the orchards yield the amount of produce the promoters claimed they would. And the climate, though ideal for many things including recuperative tuberculosis patients, was far from ideal for fruit farming. But it is doubtful that these claims were made with any deliberate attempt to mislead the buyer. The BCDA, with its singular lack of knowledge about British Columbia may have honestly believed that the climate was "ideal." It no doubt fully intended to establish a horticultural school when the opportunity arose. And though some chroniclers unfortunately made much of the fact that the pictures of mature fruit-laden trees used for advertising purposes were actually pictures of orchards in the Okanagan valley and not in Walhachin, the use of these pictures did not necessarily mean that the company was being deliberately deceptive. The use of pictures of other orchards was almost to be expected for at the time that the advertising campaign was at its peak, the trees at Walhachin were only seedlings. And for the directors of a company 6,000 miles away to assume that the soil and climate conditions of orchards in the Okanagan, just a few hundred miles distant from Walhachin would be reasonably similar, was not surprising.

The BCDA's assurance to the potential buyer that his orchard holdings would be financially rewarding cannot be branded as being deliberately misleading either, because one must remember that the general feeling of the day was that orchard farming provided a sure route to wealth, and that the best place in the world to start an orchard was in British Columbia.

"The wonderful bench lands of the Thompson River," Premier Sir Richard McBride told the British Columbia Legislature in March, 1910, as reported in the Inland Sentinel, "the lands of the dry belt as well as those outside . . . are only in the infancy of their development. It is amazing to find from investigation of those technically proficient to speak with authority, that their conclusions as to the wealth of the soil in this particular region of British Columbia are in the very highest degree favorable."

On March 18, 1910, the same paper, reporting on proceedings in the House of Commons, stated, ". . . The greater part of the time of the House yesterday was taken up with an argument between Martin Burrell, Member for Yale-Cariboo, and the honorable Member from Nova Scotia as to the relative merits of British Columbian and Nova Scotian fruit. Mr. Goodeve, (Kootenay) backed up British Columbia's position by pointing to the array of medals won in England and elsewhere by British Columbian fruit."

Two weeks previously, a British Columbia apple grower, A.L. Morris, had informed the Inland Sentinel that he had received a letter from King Edward VII acknowledging a box of apples that Morris had sent as a gift. According to the newspaper report, the letter from Windsor Castle stated that since the king did not eat "gifts," a cheque was enclosed for twenty dollars to pay for the apples. Morris ventured the opinion that if the King of England felt that British Columbia apples were worth twenty dollars a box instead of the usual three dollars, then the question of which province in Canada produced the finest fruit was settled for all time.

That same spring J.C. Metcalfe, commissioner of marketing

First section of land tilled and ready for seeding.

for the British Columbia government, explained in the British Columbia Legislature that Manitoba could expect to receive no shipments of fruit in 1910 because Alberta and Saskatchewan would require all the available produce. "This," he explained, "is not because of any scarcity in the crop, but because the market for British Columbia fruit is growing too big to handle."[5]

    As historian Mary Balf points out, Canada's Governor General Earl Grey gave an unexpected stamp of approval to the

British Columbia fruit industry when, in opening the 1910 New Westminster Fruit Exhibition in London, he publicly stated that British Columbia offered ". . . the opportunity of living under such ideal conditions as struggling humanity has only succeeded in reaching in one or two of the most favored parts of the earth."[6]

Almost simultaneously, the British Columbia government announced that it would establish five demonstration orchards in the province, one of which was to be located either at Savona or at Walhachin, the two being only twelve miles (19 kilometers) apart.[7]

In the light of such enthusiasm it is no wonder orchard enterprises anywhere in the province of British Columbia were looked upon with favor, nor is it at all surprising that the sale of shares in Walhachin proceeded at a steady rate.

"The fact that the Company is cultivating a large portion of the land for itself," the BCDA brochure confidently declared, "besides reserving to itself more than two-hundred acres of the planted orchard land . . . is the best evidence of the confidence the Company has in the value of these lands as a business investment."

"It is impossible to over-estimate the importance of the railway facilities right in the settlement," the brochure went on, extolling the fact that both the Canadian Pacific and the Canadian National Railways ran through the orchard area. "This renders Walhachin unique among fruit growing properties in the Dry Belt of British Columbia."

Much was also made of the fact that the land in question lay along the banks of the Thompson River. However, the fact that the orchard fields sat at an elevation of 1,100 feet above the level of the river, at a time when the hydraulic lifting of water was financially impractical, was virtually ignored. And, rather than crediting the obvious disadvantages of such a location, the brochure indirectly implied that the elevation was a decided advantage to the settlers because of the health benefits that would result from such high and dry air.

However, here again it is impossible to be overly critical of the BCDA. Whether this action was done out of ignorance, or whether the excessive elevation was being deliberately played down, is open to conjecture. Certainly, neither Ashcroft nor Palmer, the engineer and the agriculturalist who were asked to assess the potential of the area before the BCDA decided to go ahead with its investment, made any mention of the possible disadvantages of the height of the fields above the only readily available water supply. Consequently, it is not surprising that the company located 6,000 miles away in London should have failed to recognize the seriousness of the situation.

In any event, the advertising was successful. The project caught the fancy of many upper-class English families and no one asked any embarrassing questions.

Both five-acre and ten-acre lots were offered for sale, but most prospective buyers chose ten-acre holdings. The price for these holdings was listed in the brochure as $3,500 and up for planted land or $3,000 and up for unplanted land, though when the orchardists arrived on the spot they found there was a considerable difference in prices. There was such a diversity of soil conditions throughout the 5,000-acre area, and so much of the land was unsuited for agriculture of any kind, that an acre could sell for anything from $250 (considerably less than the brochure stated) to as much as $1,500, depending on its location.

The BCDA brochure also advertised that houses could be ready for occupancy when the settlers arrived. A four-room house, painted and with a bath, was offered at $1,100, while those people who wished larger houses could have additional rooms built at the price of $125 per room.

Payment terms were also available. Purchasers could divide the total price into four yearly installments with an annual interest fee of six per cent added to the outstanding balance. Also, if anyone wished to delay his arrival — this clause was principally intended, in the words of the brochure, for ". . . English public school boys undergoing a course of preliminary training in Horticultural schools prior to taking up their land" — but still wished to have his ten-acre holding planted and started on its four to six-year growth period depending on the species of apple planted, then the BCDA also offered to manage any acreage for a nominal annual fee paid in advance, until such time as that purchaser was ready to establish himself as a permanent resident of the settlement.

Transportation was also arranged. The steamship fare from Liverpool to Montreal was quoted as ninety dollars first class, forty dollars second class, or twenty-five dollars third class. The rail fare from Montreal to Walhachin was either eighty dollars or thirty-five dollars, depending whether one chose to travel first class or colonist.

The BCDA also managed to win from the government the concession that all settlers' effects would be admitted duty-free into Canada. This concession was a surprisingly important factor in convincing many ambivalent investors about British

16

Columbia, for the absence of customs duties meant investors could bring with them all their household china, silver, linens, ornate carved furniture and other "objets d'art" without which they would have hesitated to emigrate to the Canadian wilderness. For in setting out to attract only upper-class Englishmen to its Walhachin venture, the BCDA had been even more successful than it had hoped. Not only were the original orchardists, without exception, members of upper-class English families, but many were also titled members of the aristocracy. Among the orchardists were included descendants of Prime Minister Lord Asquith, Lord Nelson, King George V and Cecil Rhodes.[8]

This was really not surprising when one considers that the shareholders of the London-based BCDA carried out most of the original promotion of the Walhachin venture among their own friends and business associates and, as Riis points out, ". . . an examination of the lists of shareholders of the BCDA reveals that seventy per cent list their occupation as either gentleman or knight, and another twenty-eight per cent refer to themselves as barrister and solicitor, or by some military rank." Accordingly, it is to be expected the people to whom these upper-class shareholders would talk about their new orchard enterprise, and the people they would contact about the possibility of buying a share in the venture, would be people who belonged to the same upper-class level of society.

Footnotes:

[1]Nelson A. Riis, "Settlement Abandonment — A Case Study of Walhachin." Unpublished Master's Thesis, Department of Geography, University of British Columbia, 1970.

[2]Ibid.

[3]Mary Balf, *A History of the District to 1914.* Kamloops: Kamloops Museum Association, 1969.

[4]Walhachin promotion brochure.

[5]Inland Sentinel, Kamloops, B.C. June 11, 1910.

[6]Mary Balf, *A History of the District to 1914.* Kamloops: Kamloops Museum Association, 1969.

[7]Inland Sentinel, Kamloops, B.C. March 22, 1910.
It should be noted here, although these experimental orchards were not developed until years later than suggested in this news report, this fact did not alter the effect this announcement had on public opinion at the time the news report was made public.

[8]Nelson A. Riis, "Settlement Abandonment — A Case Study of Walhachin." Unpublished Master's Thesis, Department of Geography, University of British Columbia, 1970.

Nothing is Impossible

Close-up view of the flume trough.

Walhachin lies in the centre of the Dry Belt of British Columbia. The annual rainfall is estimated to be approximately 7.55 inches (nineteen centimeters) almost exactly the same as Reno, Nevada, and Phoenix, Arizona, and about one-tenth the rainfall received in the Vancouver area. In Walhachin during the months of June, July, and August, temperatures of one-hundred degrees Fahrenheit (thirty-eight degrees Celsius) are not uncommon. Even April and May may see several weeks of ninety degrees Fahrenheit (thirty-two degrees Celsius) weather. And although the directors of the London-based BCDA and its advertising promoters were seemingly unconcerned about this hot and dry climate along the Thompson River benches, and quite unperturbed about the lack of available water for irrigation purposes, Charles Barnes and the British Columbia

18

View of Barnes Estates showing lateral system.

Horticultural Estates Company, who were on the spot, were not.

Soil analysis had indicated that the acreage the company bought would grow a wide variety of produce provided it received sufficient moisture. But a total of 7.55 inches (nineteen centimeters) of rainfall annually was far from sufficient. And the fields would receive no water from the river without the construction of an elaborate hydraulic pumping system which would be economically impossible. Accordingly, the British Columbia Horticultural Estates Company now concentrated on finding some way to provide a constant and inexpensive source of water for its five thousand acres.

One thousand of these acres lay on the south shore of the river. This property had a limited water supply from Twin Lakes, Brassey Creek, Jimmie Creek and Upper Ranch Creek which

was sufficient to supply the needs of the townsite and to irrigate those small sections of orchard which lay adjacent to each of the creek beds. But, on the north shore where the bulk of the orchard fields lay, there was no water supply. As a result, Barnes instituted a diligent search of the hills which lay behind the fields on this northern bank. Finally, some twenty miles (32 kilometers) away at Deadman's Creek, Barnes found what he was looking for — a fresh free-flowing creek which was fed by underground springs. But the problem was to devise a means of carrying a steady flow of water the twenty-mile (32 kilometer) distance back to Walhachin.

The method Barnes and his orchardists finally settled on to achieve this was by the construction of a wooden flume or trough, six feet wide and thirty inches deep supported on

Construction being done on a section of canal.

wooden trestles which snaked down the mountainside carrying a gravity-propelled flow of water to a series of irrigation ditches which would be dug between the rows of apple trees. It was an ambitious project — one which demanded a commendable degree of determination and effort on the part of everyone involved: Barnes, the orchardists and the score of Chinese labourers who were hired to assist with the construction work. Unfortunately, the project was badly planned.

In building their flume the orchardists concentrated on two prime objects: first, speed of completion, and second, economy. They were determined to provide adequate irrigation for the fields as rapidly as possible, since at best it would be four years before any trees could produce fruit and these trees would be only the Wagoners and the Jonathons. The Rome Beauty's, the

A section of the main flume, showing a connecting lateral flume, and an open spillway for volume control.

A work party in the fields.

Wealthy's and the other varieties all required five or six years to mature. Understandably, the orchardists had no wish to delay this maturing date an extra year because they delayed their planting for a whole season while they leisurely constructed their irrigation system.

Their second objective, to complete the construction as economically as possible, was equally important in their thinking. The BCDA had taken out a large bank loan to finance the original purchase of the orchard property. In addition, the BCDA had financed the cost of clearing and preparing the soil, the purchase of some 35,000 seedling trees from nurseries in the United States, the laying out of the townsite and the construction of roads. This company had little desire to go deeper into debt. Certainly, the orchardists would eventually

pay back the BCDA for money spent on the construction of the flume and the irrigation ditches through the instigation of water charges, but in the meantime the London-based company was responsible for providing it. And the orchardists themselves, were equally eager to keep building expenses to a minimum. They faced an immediate four or five-year term when they could expect to receive no return from their fruit trees. Their only source of income would be from the sale of potatoes, tomatoes and onions which they would plant as "intermediate" crops between the rows of growing seedling trees, and these crops would provide little more than living expenses. In addition, each orchardist was already being assessed an annual water fee of four dollars on each acre he owned, and he was fairly certain that this water fee would be immediately increased if the cost of the

Seedling trees being planted.

Four-furrow irrigation system between the rows of seedling trees.

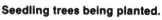

construction of the flume and the irrigation ditches was more than the directors of the BCDA had anticipated. Accordingly, the orchardists were determined to save money in every possible way.

In just over six months, Barnes and his orchardists succeeded in completing twenty miles (32 kilometers) of flume and irrigation ditches — sufficient to irrigate the field area on the north bank of the Thompson River. And according to the Inland Sentinel of April 29, 1910, they completed this construction for a total cost of under $100,000.[1]

But the push to complete the construction in record time, had disastrous effects. Perhaps the most glaring was that it precluded their taking time to ask for professional advice. Neither the orchardists, nor the laborers employed to assist with

the work, had any knowledge of engineering, and at best they had only a rudimentary knowledge of construction work. Thus, they constructed a trough six feet wide and thirty inches deep and then placed it on shaky wooden tressles set into the rocky hillside on inadequate footings, with the result that the tressles could not support the weight of the water which the flume had been designed to carry. Having spent a sum of some $20,000[2] for sufficient lumber to construct a thirty-inch-deep trough, the orchardists now had to limit the depth of water which came down the trough to a mere six inches.

Perhaps this restricted water flow might have been adequate to supply five acre-inches of water per week, which geologists accepted as being adequate for both the soil and the climatic conditions of that particular region, but, unfortunately, the inexperience of the orchardists did not stop there. In their haste to complete the irrigation system in record time, they neglected to put a gravel lining into any of the sections of ditch which connected certain sections of the flume or which carried the water from the flume out through the fields between the rows of apple trees.

At one time the orchardists considered the possibility of lining the ditches with cement, and in one small area this was actually done, but it was not continued. As a result some forty per cent of the water which came down the flume was lost to seepage in the dry sandy soil before it reached any of the orchard trees.

The determination to economize had equally disastrous repercussions. Approximately 1,350,000 board feet of lumber for the flume and the supporting tressles were purchased from the Monarch Lumber Company in Savona, British Columbia, for a sum of $20,250.00, and all of it was reject material. No doubt if top-grade lumber had been purchased, the sum would have been considerably higher, but in this instance economy was a mistake. For by ordering "reject" lumber, the orchardists could not specify either thickness or length. They had to accept whatever was available. As a consequence, most of the boards delivered were only one inch to 1.75 inches thick, which was not thick enough to resist warping or seepage, and too thin to be properly caulked.

The consequences of this were twofold — not only was there considerable water loss, but in those spots where the leakage occurred above a supporting tressle, the seeping water weakened the already shallow footings of the tressle foundations, and in some instances gradually washed out the tressle itself.

But perhaps the most destructive result of the purchase of this reject lumber was that it led to the improper construction of the flume trough.

In order to have functioned properly, the trough should have been built in sections. Then, if one part was damaged or knocked down with the collapse of one of the tressles, it would not have affected the entire structure. However, when the orchardists were forced to make use of odds and ends of reject lumber which had different lengths and thicknesses, the construction of the flume in separate sections would have necessitated a great deal of arduous and time-consuming sawing. So instead, they elected to leave the lengths just as they were and to build an interwoven structure. They interlaced the boards throughout the whole length of the trough with the result that if one part was washed out it twisted down 100 yards or more of undamaged flume. This unnecessary damage was critical, for, while a small break was not too difficult to repair, the replacement of a large section was a tremendous undertaking, particularly if the damaged section extended over one of the countless gullies or ravines which cut into the hillside.

In 1911 an addition had to be made to the irrigation system on the south side of the river, because it was found that the water available from Twin Lakes, Brassey Creek, Jimmie Creek and Upper Ranch Creek could supply the needs of the community but was insufficient to irrigate all the orchard fields. Accordingly, it was decided to transport water from the flume on the northern bank to these 300 acres of fruit trees. In April, 1911, a steel pipe was laid across the river, but within two months it was washed out by the accumulation of debris swept downstream during run-off. A suspension bridge was then constructed, from which a six-inch steel pipe was slung. The pipe was ready for use during the summer of 1911 and continued to be used for the next three years. However, during excessively dry periods even it could not provide adequate irrigation. So, early in 1914 this steel pipe was replaced with a twelve-inch wooden one.

But these additions were not part of the original construction. The flume and the irrigation ditches which provided water to all the acreage on the north bank of the Thompson River were completed, in spite of their flaws, during the summer of 1910, in time for the fall planting season; they were ready for continuous use as soon as spring came. And this completion date was fortunate because, during the spring and the summer of 1911, more than 500 acres of seedling trees were laid out on the northern benchlands.

The fall of 1910 had seen the completion of all the planting on the southern shore, mainly as a result of Manager Barnes' acquisition of a gasoline traction plow which enabled the orchardists to break up the land and ready it for planting in record time.

"The gasolene traction plow is an unequalled success," the Inland Sentinel announced in April, 1910. "It uses about thirty gallons of gasolene per day and plows twelve furrows at one time. It can clear seventeen acres in a single day."

However, it should be noted that the report in the paper may have been more enthusiastic than truthful for by the spring of 1911 Barnes and his orchardists had elected to return to the use of horse-drawn plows for clearing the fields and digging the

furrows. Whether this change was because the traction plow used an excessive amount of gasoline, whether it demanded an expertise on the part of its users which the orchardists did not possess, or whether it was for quite a different reason, can only be speculated about.

Meantime, while many of the orchardists had been busy constructing the flume and irrigation system, and others had cleared and planted the orchard fields, Barnes' Horticultural Estates Company had been concentrating on establishing the townsite. Barnes' chief concern was to see that the incoming settlers would find their new homes as civilized and as comfortable as the advertising brochure of the BCDA would have led them to expect.

In the summer of 1908, long before any of the orchardists

View of the six-inch (fifteen-centimeter) pipe suspended across the river on a cable to provide additional water to the fields on the southern bank.

Until the completion of the government bridge in the spring of 1912, the only means of crossing the river was by ferry.

had arrived, the site of the town was surveyed. One hundred and fifty town lots were laid out and then twenty-five acres of grass were planted to counteract the desert-like appearance of the landscape. The lots fronted on a winding road which edged the river and looked down the steep cliff-like banks onto the fast-moving waters of the Thompson River. Behind the lots rose the purple sage-covered hills and a waterfall rumbled over the rocks in a narrow crag directly back of the main section of the townsite. It was a pretty setting.

Down the entire length of the main street, Barnes laid a wood-stave water pipe. The pipe was six inches in diameter, wrapped with wire to keep it tight and capable of carrying a large quantity of water. Each house or business in the settlement could hook directly into it with a length of galvanized pipe.

Roads were cleared which connected the town lots with each other and with the train station. Other roads were built which led to the various areas of orchard fields.

The next project was the construction of the houses for the incoming settlers. This project was of prime importance to Barnes because the houses had to fit into the picture of leisured, comfortable upper-class living which the BCDA had promised its investors. And here Barnes was fortunate for among the earliest group of arrivals was an Englishman named B.C. Footner, who was a competent builder. Footner seemed to appreciate the importance of constructing houses which would meet the incoming settlers' expectations and he soon became the chief designer and builder in the settlement.

The view from the townsite which overlooked the constantly changing greys, greens, and blacks of the rushing Thompson River, was spectacular. Accordingly, Footner designed each house with a large circular picture window which faced onto the river and overlooked the orchard fields on the opposite bank. This window, glassed in small square panes, sat low to the floor and reached the full height of the wall, providing the residents with a full view up and down the valley.

Then just as he had considered the importance of the view, Footner also considered the exigencies of the climate. In spite of the fact that the townsite hugged the riverbank where the houses would catch any hint of breeze, Footner knew the months of summer heat could be unpleasant, particularly for people who had recently left the cool, damp climate of England. Accordingly, he designed his houses with twelve-foot ceilings in all the main-floor rooms to allow good air circulation, and with steeply-pitched conical wood-shake rooves to provide insulation against the heat. In addition, he gave each house a wide-roofed veranda along its front and down one side, accessible from the front steps and from the inside through French doors which opened off one of the bedrooms. In some instances, notably in the stone house which Footner built for his own family, this veranda was completely screened.

The decorative touches were not ignored even in this wilderness setting. Each veranda pillar boasted a hand-carved scroll-like design where it met the roof, and the wood boards of each veranda floor were carefully laid in symmetrical patterns.

Inside the houses, comfort was Footner's prime consideration. The larger bedrooms had diagonal corner clothes closets and individual porcelain wash basins with both hot and cold running water taps. Many houses had a "receiving room" directly inside the front door where guests could wait in comfort. Every house had indoor plumbing, and either a copper or a porcelain tub sitting off the floor on four sturdy legs.

For those few orchardists who required a larger family home, Footner constructed houses with an upper storey, containing two or three extra bedrooms, and in some cases, an upstairs sun-porch which jutted out of the steeply-pitched roof.

Also, every house had a large stone fireplace in the main sitting room, a roomy and dry cement cellar, and carbide pressure lamps for lighting. Certainly, the newly-arrived residents of Walhachin had no reason to complain that Barnes and his Horticultural Estates Company had failed to live up to the promises made in the BCDA brochure to provide the same comfortable upper-class living conditions which the orchardists had left behind in England.

A steady stream of settlers was expected. By July, 1910, fifty-six had arrived from England and as many more had purchased property or were on the point of doing so. It is interesting to note that of those who arrived, about eighty per cent were between the ages of eighteen and thirty-nine.[3]

Immediately, the newcomers set to work to seed their ten-acre holdings with fruit trees, and those people who reached Walhachin early enough in the summer managed to plant potatoes and tomatoes as intermediate crops between the rows of seedling fruit trees. Those people who came too late for the growing season that year made plans for what they would plant early the following spring.

As rapidly as he could, Footner built homes to fill the orders of the new arrivals. By Christmas of 1910 he had completed thirteen houses — eleven of which were occupied while two awaited the arrival of their owners. Four more houses were in the final stages of completion. Those residents whose houses had not yet been constructed lived at the Walhachin Hotel, which was completed early in April, 1910.

"The Walhachin Hotel is delightfully laid out and furnished," the Ashcroft Journal stated July 9, 1910. "The large dining room overlooks the orchards and from the open balcony on the north side a good view is obtained of the orchards and of the Thompson River. Spacious billiard, card and ladies' and gentlemen's sitting rooms occupy the east wing. Hot and cold water, gas and all comforts have had careful attention."

Though the paper did not mention it, the hotel also boasted an attractive old-English garden, and maintained a string of carriages for the sole purpose of conducting guests on leisurely drives around the townsite and through the orchard fields.

Hotel rates were set at thirty-five dollars a month for full board and lodging. Rooms alone were ten dollars a month and any casual visitor who might want a hot bath, but who was not a registered overnight guest, could have one for a twenty-five cent fee. The dining room had established a reputation for serving excellent meals, and on Christmas Day, 1910, fifty guests sat down for Christmas dinner.

Several buildings in the townsite had been completed before the spring of 1910, including a bunkhouse for the workers, a general store and the Canadian Pacific Railway (CPR) foreman's house which had been in existence since 1906. However, the bulk of the building was done after the snow melted in 1910. One of the first buildings completed was Manager Barnes' house. It was a large wood-frame structure with four pillars in front which supported an upper balcony. The house sat on a large square piece of ground overlooking the river, completely encircled by a two-foot high stone fence.

In August, 1910, the main square of the townsite was laid out, and a road was cleared and leveled which led from the station to the new hotel. In October, 1910, the Walhachin Post Office was established with Reginald Pole as the first postmaster. The Ashcroft Journal of October 12, 1910, somewhat wryly points out that since the daily mail arrived at the settlement on a CPR train which reached Walhachin in the early hours of the morning, Pole ". . . would have to accustom himself to getting up very early."

More than a score of Chinese labourers had been employed to assist with clearing the fields and planting the seedling trees, and later in October, a Chinese laundry, was built on the low-lying land east of the townsite close to a readily available water supply. According to the Ashcroft Journal, the laundry was "overrun with orders."

In February, 1911, work began on the construction of a government bridge across the Thompson River near the old Pennie ranch site. Until this time, the only way across the river had been by ferry, and when the water was high, goods and people had to be transported by means of a cradle attached to a cable. Fortunately, both railways ran along the south shore of the river at that time, which enabled the orchardists to travel directly from Walhachin west to Ashcroft or east to Kamloops without having to cross the river. However, with 4,000 of their 5,000 acres of orchard on the northern bank, as well as the flume and the greater proportion of the system of irrigation ditches, trips from the townsite across the river to the northern bench lands were constant necessities. Therefore, the completion of a bridge was awaited with great impatience. Unfortunately, work was delayed the entire summer of 1911 because of unusually high water. But finally, early the following spring the government bridge was completed, and the residents of Walhachin had good reason to feel they had finally moved into modern times.

In May, 1911, a barber, Mr. Skentelberg arrived from England. He set up his shop and he also, according to the Ashcroft Journal, "found that business was booming." The Walhachin Restaurant opened for business two months later. Meals were advertised for thirty-five cents, or for twenty-five cents if they were purchased in a book of twenty-one tickets.

By Christmas, 1911, only a little more than eighteen months after the first settlers had arrived, there were 180 permanent residents in Walhachin[4] — 107 of these settlers were English orchardists and their families. The rest were the families of CPR personel, construction workers, people hired on the various Horticultural Estates Company projects, which included the poultry farm and the ranch, and a handful of domestic servants who came with their mistresses from England. In addition, there were the Chinese workers whom the company employed to assist with the work in the fields.

By now the townsite had now grown to include the Walhachin Hotel, the general store, a butcher shop, three laundries, a bakery and tea room, a dairy, a livery stable, a ladies's store, a wood and coal yard, two insurance offices and a post office.

Orchard land was being cleared at a rate of more than 250 acres each season, at first with the help of Barnes' traction plow, later with teams of horses and then in 1912 with six steam tractors newly purchased by the company. With the new steam tractors work progressed much more rapidly for they were both inexpensive to run and efficient.

As 1911 drew to a close, it appeared that Walhachin was living up to all the expectations of its promoters. The townsite was well established, living conditions were comfortable with running water and carbide lighting in all the houses, the irrigation system was working reasonably well and more and more acres of land were being put under cultivation each year. In the light of all these developments, it is surprising that on June 12, 1912 the London-based BCDA removed its financial support from the project. The BCDA announced that no additional investment

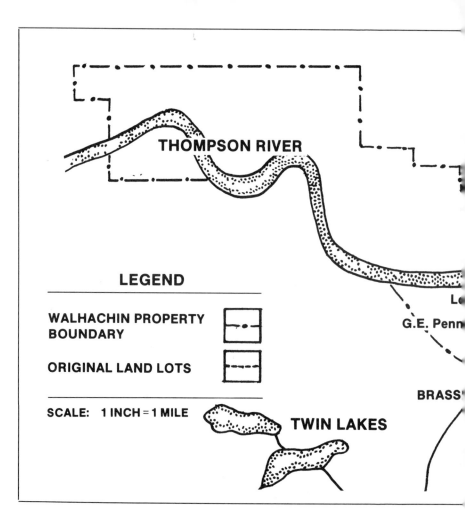

LEGEND

WALHACHIN PROPERTY BOUNDARY

ORIGINAL LAND LOTS

SCALE: 1 INCH = 1 MILE

THOMPSON RIVER

G.E. Penn

BRASS

TWIN LAKES

would be considered, and advised its shareholders to sell their shares and attempt to recover as much as they could from their original investments.

Fortunately for the orchardists at Walhachin, a new financial backer emerged in the person of the 6th Marquis of Angelsey. As the BCDA relinquished its control, the Marquis bought up the Walhachin holdings. Gradually he assumed financial control of the British Columbia Horticultural Estates Company, the Dry Belt Settlement Company and all the subsidiary companies which had been developed. He even assumed financial control of the Walhachin Hotel.

In the summer of 1912, the Marquis came to Walhachin and began construction on his own estate, "Angelsey," situated some three miles along the river west of the townsite, on the northern bank.

34

ORIGINAL LAND LOTS

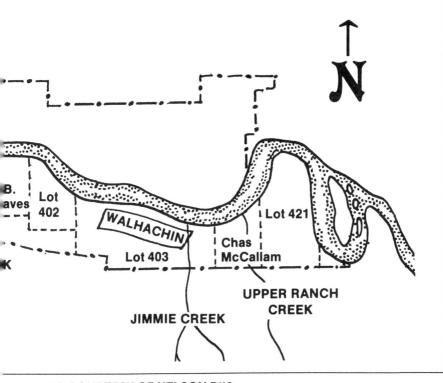

MAP COURTESY OF NELSON RIIS

Two widely discussed actions the Marquis took shortly after his arrival were strangely at odds with each other. The first concerned the Walhachin Hotel whose ownership he had just assumed. Until that time it had been an established custom for the hotel, in both its dining room and its beverage rooms, to cater only to "upper-class" clientelle. The Marquis took exception to this ruling. Instead, he insisted that from then on the hotel would serve any customer, from whatever walk of life, who wished to patronize it.

But his second action was sadly at variance. Early in the spring of 1913, after he completed his new house at "Angelsey," the Marquis proceeded to construct a cement-lined swimming pool directly adjacent to his house and linked to it with a wide cement walk. He then allowed none but the titled and the most aristocratic members of the Walhachin community to make use of his pool.

But despite this act of restricting the use of his pool to the titled few, the Marquis was found to be friendly, unassuming and hard-working by the other residents of the orchard community. In fact, he was regarded as being surprisingly free from the arrogance which was an unfortunate characteristic of so many of his peers. Unfortunately, the orchard residents did not say the same of Lady Angelsey, but since her visits to Walhachin were infrequent and of short duration, perhaps the reports about her were somewhat biased.

In some respects, however, the change of financial ownership of the orchard community from the hands of the shareholders of the BCDA into the hands of the Marquis of Angelsey may not have been entirely for the good. Though he worked in the fields alongside his men in overalls and heavy boots, it is doubtful that the Marquis knew much about orchard production. Nor did he display any great knowledge of basic engineering. Early in 1914 the Marquis acquired a new section of land on the south shore of the river, east of the townsite — Lot 421. The already inadequate supply of water available on this south side of the Thompson could not be stretched to include any new areas, but the Marquis wanted his property properly irrigated. Accordingly, it was his urging which resulted in the decision by the orchardists to replace the six-inch steel pipe suspended across the river on a cable, with a large twelve-inch wooden one. In fact, the Marquis himself put up the $7,250 needed to finance it. But again lack of expertise resulted in a waste of effort and money. The Marquis should have consulted someone with practical experience before spending all that money to suspend a wooden water pipe across a river on a suspension cable unable to support its weight. Over the whole of the growing season, the Marquis' new pipe provided less water than the smaller six-inch pipe had done. Certainly the wooden pipe was capable of carrying a far larger volume, but the weight of this additional water, added to the weight of the pipe itself, caused the suspension cable to sag until it was just above river level. The moment the river rose during spring run-off and all during the weeks of high water, the use of this pipe had to be discontinued. It had to be cleared of water completely. Otherwise, it would have been submerged and washed away in a matter of moments under the force of the swiftly moving Thompson River.

In another area, too, the Marquis' influence was questionable. Immediately after World War I he replaced Charles Barnes in the position of manager of the British Columbia Horticultural Estates Company with Ralph Chetwynd — this action had serious effects on the ultimate future of the settlement.

Barnes was a man of tremendous energy and determination who had been committed to the orchard dream from its inception — a man with proven leadership qualities who had earned the respect and the admiration of every orchardist in the settlement. Chetwynd had celebrated his "coming of age" at a dance his mother gave in Walhachin in August, 1911. Granted "Rafe" Chetwynd, as he was affectionately called by everyone who knew him, was popular. Granted he had proved his ability on the battlefield during the course of World War I. But, in 1919 when the orchard settlement was on the verge of collapse, strong leadership was essential, and Chetwynd was still too young to command the respect of his fellow orchardists, and too inexperienced to deal with the problems of such a diverse polyglot community.[4]

Footnotes:

[1]Nelson A. Riis, "Settlement Abandonment — A Case Study of Walhachin." Unpublished Master's Thesis, Department of Geography, University of British Columbia. 1970.

[2]Ibid.

[3]Ibid.

[4]Ibid.

A Way of Life

The hotel dining room where dinner guests wore formal evening clothes.

The Walhachin Hotel, which for many of the early orcha

The growth of the social life at Walhachin kept pace with the economic development, and the social standard maintained was one of the most remarkable characteristics of the settlement.

The hotel, completed early in the spring of 1910 and officially opened during one of Sir Wilfred Laurier's trips west, was reputed to be the most luxurious hotel in the area. It had hot and cold running water, indoor plumbing and steam heating. The gardens outside were laid out in picturesque old-English style, and both motors and democrats were available to be hired for scenic drives around the settlement.

The hotel was constantly filled, for it was a lodging place not only for the unmarried orchardists, but also for the constant flow of guests who came from England. For Walhachin had been discovered to be a remarkable place for grouse shooting and

pleted early in 1910, was "home"

fishing, and friends and relatives of the orchardists came in great
numbers to take advantage of the sport. These guests were so
numerous that in 1911 additional rooms were built, and an ad
was run in the Ashcroft Journal appealing for extra waitresses to
serve the constantly growing clientele who patronized the dining
room. The tone established in the hotel was everything Manager
Barnes could have wished. To appear for dinner there in
anything but acceptable evening dress was as much a social
solecism in Walhachin as it would have been in Mayfair. And
though the regular clientele numbered little more than 100
people, the hotel maintained two separate beverage rooms so
that anyone coming in for a drink who was casually dressed need
not offend those patrons who were properly attired.

Women, as well as men were accepted without comment as

39

May 24th festivities.

patrons of the "formal" beverage room, for it was regarded as being no different from one of the exclusive London clubs. And though women were always a minority in the settlement — there were only fifteen in 1910 and still fewer than fifty when World War I broke out — nevertheless, afternoon tea was an established custom. From the time Miss Eleanor Flowerdew took over the duties of housekeeper at the hotel in early 1910, until the English orchardists abandoned the settlement, afternoon tea was served daily in the dining room. No matter how hot or how cold the weather, the ladies of Walhachin turned out in their finest dresses and bonnets to socialize around tea tables set with crisply starched linen clothes and decorated in the summer months with individual bouquets of freshly picked garden flowers, or with sprigs of sage and potted violets in the winter.

Card parties, often with high stakes, were held weekly, both in private homes and in the hotel and these card parties, too, attracted the women as well as the men. Such entertainments had been customary for women in England since the time of Jane Austen. But unfortunately, many of the residents of the surrounding towns of Ashcroft and Savona did not realize this fact. The "gambling" parties at Walhachin, and particularly the participation of the women, received a great deal of criticism. But that criticism in no way spoiled the enjoyment of the orchardists. In fact, the English population of Walhachin cared little for the opinion of their "colonial" neighbors.

In addition to the card parties, there were musical evenings and concerts at which everyone took a turn. The lists of selections included vocal numbers, duets, piano selections and

41

A family outing.

instrumental numbers performed by a varied list of orchardists. And a comparison of the names on the lists of arrivals with those names on the weekly concert programs reveals that new-comers were promptly invited to share their talents with the rest of the residents.

Several times a month a ball was held, in the hotel during the early years, and later, after its completion, in the community hall. And in spite of the 6,000 miles which separated Walhachin from civilized English society, the calibre of the dancing at these balls was not allowed to become unfashionably rural. Miss Ivatt, whose family had come to Walhachin in early 1910, organized a series of dancing classes which, according to reports published in local papers, were attended by "a surprisingly large number of residents." Mrs. Al Faucault or Mrs. Charles Barnes provided

The skating rink.

music for the balls, with one of half a dozen others ready to take over if these two should get tired. And as a last resort, a gramophone was available. Dress was strictly formal, and every gathering concluded with the singing of *Auld Lang Syne, God Save the King* and *America*, the last no doubt a concession to the popular orchard manager, Charles Barnes.

It is a reflection of the esteem in which the orchard residents held their American-born manager, that they should have agreed to include a salute to his country along with one to their own and this esteem was not misplaced. Barnes had undoubtedly been the driving force behind the early development of the settlement. The only non-Englishman in the original group, he was reputed to have made it a custom to stride around the property in a pair of tweed knickers and a tweed cap which made it impossible to tell him from one of the titled gentry with whom he rubbed shoulders. Nor did his manners reveal any lack of polish. He was as much a "gentleman" as any one of those who bore a title.

The number of guests constantly in evidence in the settlement was rather remarkable, particularly when it lay in such a relatively isolated situation. However, not only did large numbers of guests come from England to enjoy the hunting and the fishing, but friends from Vancouver and Kamloops were often invited to attend one of the balls. They came to the orchard settlement by train, attended the dance, stayed overnight at the hotel and then returned home by train. However, it should be pointed out here that these so-called "colonial" guests were never numerous and they invariably belonged to the highest level of society. In fact, many of these guests were connected in some way with the titled families at Walhachin. Ordinary middle-class people, were not invited, nor were the working class. Even those working-class residents of Walhachin itself — those people who ran the poultry ranch, the cowboys who looked after the cattle and the CPR personnel — were strictly excluded from these formal affairs.

Those guests who were "honored" with an invitation to attend a ball at Walhachin, like their hosts and hostesses, came dressed in their most formal attire — fashionable evening dresses for the ladies and dinner jackets, top hats, white gloves and canes for the gentlemen. One local resident, whom the Chetwynds invited to a dance, arrived in Walhachin on the train only to discover she had neglected to pack her long white evening gloves. This mistake was almost enough to compel her to remain hidden in the hotel and to miss the ball entirely, except that such an action would have been an insult to her hosts. Besides, she knew that the manners of the orchardists were far too perfect to allow anyone to show any disdain or to comment on her solecism. However, she made sure not to commit such a *faux pas* again.

But though the dress at the balls was formal, there was nothing stiff about the festivities. Some affairs, notably the annual Bachelors' Ball and a Spinsters's Ball held February 29, 1912, were the reverse. In fact, the Ashcroft Journal felt compelled to point out somewhat dryly that on these particular occasions the festivities could be expected to continue until after four o'clock in the morning.

There were also elaborate fancy dress balls for which the orchardists spared no effort to provide themselves with surprisingly original costumes. The list of prize-winning costumes at the ball held on Valentine's Day, 1911, included Mary Queen of Scots, a Roman Centurian, Lord Nelson, Lady Hamilton, Portia, Alice in Wonderland and Uncle Sam.

Elaborate refreshments were always provided, and for those people who despite Miss Ivatt's dancing lessons still felt the need for a break, pool and billiards were offered as a diversion.

And despite the preponderance of parties, dances and concerts, the spiritual side of life at Walhachin was not ignored. Every Sunday church services were held, conducted by the reverend Charles Venables, Anglican vicar at Ashcroft, and later by his successor, the reverend Mr. Reeves. Church rolls show there were invariably forty or more Walhachin residents in attendance at every service. At first these services were held in the hotel, but they were moved to the community hall after its completion.

In 1912 and 1913 a strong move was made to begin collecting funds to finance the building of a church. It is interesting to note that there was considerable disagreement over this particular issue. In fact, the editors of the two short-lived Walhachin newspapers, the *Chronicle* and the *Times*, both devoted editorial space to debating the issue. The *Chronicle* supported the idea, while the *Times* took a firm stand that since the new hall had just been completed and services could be held there, that the construction of a church would be expensive and unnecessary. One cannot help speculating about the priorities and biases of that same *Times* editor because in another column of the same paper he made a plea for money to upgrade the condition of the golf course and he strongly argued in defense of the "relatively minor" expense of outfitting people for polo.

But if the numbers of balls, parties, teas, concerts and card evenings in the fledgling community were prodigious, sporting events were even more numerous. A tennis club was formed in the summer of 1910 and a court was built with such proficiency that it was still in playing condition twenty years later. For the club tournament the following summer twenty-four singles players registered. A field was cleared near the poultry ranch for polo games and another area was groomed for golf. With the urging of the *Times* editor the orchardists made a push to improve the condition of the golf course, and the Walhachin Golf Club Silver Medal, awarded to the winner of the golf tournaments, is still on display in the Kamloops Museum.

The orchardists even managed to stage fox hunts. The fact that the Thompson River valley contained a singular paucity of foxes did nothing to deter the ardent huntsmen. They merely cast coyotes, of which there were more than enough, in the central role. However, in this instance, as in so many of their business enterprises, the orchardists' inexperience with frontier living was conspicuous, though it was not due entirely to their own short-sightedness. On the occasion of their first "fox" hunt, as had happened with a number of more important issues, the orchardists were misled by people who might well have known better.

When the English huntsmen had originally conceived the scheme of instituting fox hunting in Walhachin by employing coyotes in the lead role, they had decided that a private stock of coyotes should be maintained. According to a newspaper interview with Kamloops old-timer Walter Brennan, published in the Kamloops Sentinel, the orchardists arranged for a local rancher to raise coyotes for this purpose. The rancher found a coyote pup, took him to his ranch and kept him until he was sufficiently grown. Then the date of the hunt was set.

The English huntsmen turned out in full regalia, properly attired and suitably mounted, with an accompanying pack of hounds and the traditional bugler. Meantime, the rancher had arranged for one of his men to use a democrat to take the coyote into the hills some distance from Walhachin, and on a pre-arranged signal, to set him free.

The huntsmen assembled, the hounds were unleashed and the bugler gave the signal. The ranchhand released the coyote and somewhat sadly, watched him race off into the sagebrush-covered hills. He returned to the ranch and tried to ignore the baying of the hounds in the distance, but the picture of what he knew was about to happen kept coming into his mind.

But as he pulled up his horses outside the barn, there stood the coyote pup cheerfully waiting to be let back into his "home."

The hunt had been a failure, but at least the English orchardists had learned something about the behavior of wild animals that had been raised as tame ones — something that the Canadian rancher should have told them in the first place, and thereafter, on the few occasions when the orchardists held other fox hunts, they took care to use wild coyotes caught just a day or two before the hunt began.

With the more traditional sports which did not have to be adapted to suit the conditions of Walhachin, the orchardists were more successful.

In 1910 the Walhachin Football Club was formed with the Duke of Argull as honorary president. A football field was prepared on the Walhachin property and the orchard community hosted and entertained the visiting clubs. It is perhaps fitting that the uniforms this settlement of titled Englishmen chose for their football team were a stately navy blue with jerseys, knickers and stocking all matching.

The Walhachin Cricket team, as would be expected, was top rank and won all its games with neighboring cricketers. In the words of the Ashcroft Journal July 11, 1910, "Walhachin plays great cricket."

In the fall months hunting and fishing trips were organized into the Cariboo. Then as the weather grew colder skating and curling took over as favorite pastimes. Since the river flowed too quickly to freeze in anything but the severest weather, a skating rink was prepared and maintained at the eastern end of the townsite, and in the fall of 1911 a hockey team was formed, probably at the invitation of those surrounding centres who were being defeated regularly at polo, football and cricket and who were looking for a chance to get revenge. A curling club was also started. The hills surrounding the town were the scenes of sleigh-riding and tobogganing parties and when the weather was too cold even for these traditional winter activities, the large billiard room in the hotel was put to use and billiard tournaments were organized.

However, not everyone remained at Walhachin during the long cold winter months. Many of the more well-to-do orchardists spent their winters back home in Britain, or in the case of the Chetwynds and the Barnes, touring Italy and France. And a steadily increasing number of bachelors put their winters to good use as they returned to England to collect their brides. The lists of arrivals at Walhachin early in March each year contain the names of a refreshing number of newly-married ladies.

And though they were now some 6,000 miles away from their homeland, the English residents of Walhachin were still the devoted servants of their King. On the occasion of the Coronation of King George V in June, 1911, an all-day celebration was held in the orchard settlement, which included horse racing, tug-of-wars, footraces and culminated in an elaborate ball in the evening. At the climax, a display of fireworks was set off, and as the strains of the national anthem died away a huge bonfire was lit, which was kept burning on the hillside behind the townsite until dawn.

It was this love of England, and the fact that almost all of the orchardists had military connections of some kind with regiments in England, that prompted the formation of the Walhachin company of the British Columbia Horse in the summer of 1911. Regular drills and parades were started in the fields which surrounded the settlement, and the more than twenty members of the Walhachin Company of the 31st British Columbia Horse were regular participants in the annual summer cavalry training camps held in Vernon. At the annual camp held in June, 1912, the Ashcroft Journal reported that the two men singled out for outstanding performance were from Walhachin — Gordon Flowerdew and Ralph Chetwynd. Both men established records in shooting competitions and in steeple-chasing. It is perhaps particularly significant that both men were also reported to have demonstrated outstanding proficiency in the Victoria Cross Race.

This was Britain's newest order of bravery, having been created by Queen Victoria specifically to honor acts of valor in the Crimean War. The first recipient, Alexander Robert Dunn, was honored for valor at Balaclava in the "Charge of the Light Brigade."

In typically British fashion, the military soon brought this new order of bravery into the world of every-day use. In addition to the regular games and contests military personnel enjoyed at training camps and on sports days, a new Victoria Cross Race was devised.[1]

The race was staged in a large field. On opposite sides at one end of the field, were heaped boards, boxes and other obstacles. Farther along, two large wagons were unhitched from their teams and turned on their sides. And at the other end of the field, standing guard over the whole area, was a formidable-looking cannon. Directly in front of the cannon and only some twenty feet away lay a life-sized dummy stretched on the ground. Directly behind the cannon stood the men in charge of firing it. Directly behind the piled up boxes and overturned wagons stood platoons of riflemen, their rifles ready.

The point of the race was for the contestants to enter the field on horseback at the opposite end from where the cannon stood waiting. Then amid the crashing of the big gun and the smoke and noise from the riflemen, they had to ride past the piles of boxes and the overturned wagons directly toward the cannon and rescue their wounded comrade.

The race was not as easy as it sounded, for though the cavalry men knew the cannon and the troopers' rifles were only loaded with blank ammunition, their horses did not. And it required considerable horsemanship to come within a mere twenty feet of that crashing gun. It was particularly difficult if the horse being ridden had taken part in a Victoria Cross Race before. The cavalryman who succeeded in finding a mount old and tired enough not to rebel, and also perhaps slightly deaf, had a distinct advantage.

It is interesting to note that it was particularly for their performance in this Victoria Race that Flowerdew and Chetwynd received special mention, since within six years of this Vernon training camp both men were decorated for bravery in World War I.

Both men were among the twenty original members of the Walhachin company of the British Columbia Horse and both went overseas in August, 1914. Ralph Chetwynd was awarded the Military Cross and recommended for the Distinguished Service Order during the final year of the war for his action in rescuing his wounded colonel and carrying him a distance of two miles through enemy fire to safety.

Gordon Flowerdew was awarded the Victoria Cross for his action during a cavalry charge northeast of the Bois de Moreuil in France on March 31, 1918. It was Easter Sunday, the day following Lieutenant Flowerdew's return to the lines after leave in England. He died two days later as a result of the wounds he received. The citation published in the London Gazette April 24, 1918, read as follows:

"For most conspicuous bravery and dash when in command of a squadron detailed for special service of a very important nature.

"On reaching the first objective, Lieutenant Flowerdew saw two lines of the enemy, each about sixty strong, with machine-guns in the centre and flanks, one line being about two hundred yards behind the other. Realising the critical nature of the operation and how much depended upon it, Lieutenant Flowerdew ordered a troop under Lieutenant Harvie, V.C. to dismount and carry out a special movement while he led the remaining three troops to the charge. The squadron (less one troop) passed over both lines, killing many of the enemy with the sword, and wheeling about galloped at them again. Although the squadron had then lost about seventy per cent of its numbers, killed and wounded, from rifle and machine-gun fire directed on it from the front and both flanks, the enemy broke and retired. The survivors of the squadron then established themselves in a position where they were joined after much hand to hand fighting by Lieutenant Harvie's party. Lieutenant Flowerdew was danger-ously wounded through both thighs during the operation, but continued to cheer on his men. There can be no doubt that this officer's great valor was the prime factor in the capture of the position."

In an interview reported in the Vancouver Province[2] in December, 1932, Major General J.E.B. Seely, C.B., C.M.G., D.S.O., sketched in an interesting background to Flowerdew's heroism. Seely had been the commander of the Canadian Cavalry Brigade and at one time the Secretary of State for War. For a short period Flowerdew had been attached to Major General Seely's brigade headquarters. And following Flowerdew's death, these excerpts from his diary were made public:

"General Seely said to me, 'Would you like to win the V.C.?' and I replied, 'That is just what my father asked me. Yes, sir, I would. It has always been my dream. But I shall never be brave enough to win it. Valor has reached such a standard that you have to be dead before you win the V.C.' "

"November 20, 1917: The great day has come and I am back with my squadron wondering whether I shall get my V.C."

"November 24, 1917: Our position is being taken over by the infantry. No chance of my V.C. this time."

A later entry read:

"General Seely said the only chance of overwhelming the Germans was to attack them on the flank as well as in front."

Perhaps it was this advice Flowerdew was remembering in his action at Moreuil Wood.

Footnotes:

[1] Sir William Denny: The Law Marches West.

[2] Interview by the Vancouver Province's London correspondent, Lukin Johnston, published in the Vancouver Sunday Province, December 11, 1932.

Entrepreneurs Par Excellence

Large clay tennis court on the Anglesey estate.

The majority of the original group of orchardists who came to Walhachin were from the upper classes of English society. Many had family titles. Many others held military ranks. But, even within this "select" group there was an unfortunate class distinction. Those settlers who were direct descendants from titled English families were conscious of their superiority. And just as the whole settlement tended to hold itself aloof from relationships with people in any of the surrounding areas, so these highest-born orchardists held themselves slightly aloof from their fellows who had not been quite as well born.

In the eyes of the "select" group, some members of the orchard community were rather "inferior" types. This included the young men who had been sent to Walhachin because they were embarrassments to their families at home. Most of these

Private swimming pool on Lord Anglesey's estate constructed in 1912. The cement foundation is still intact some seventy years later, as is a cement walk once lined with flowering shrubs which provided the swimmers with a comfortable path through the sandy soil from the pool to the house itself.

men were just out of their teens and were supported by family money. In some instances, in addition to being non-achievers, these young men had been considered by their families to be troublemakers and they had been sent to the orchard settlement as a disciplinary measure. This had been said to have been the case with a nephew of Cecil Rhodes, who arrived in Walhachin in May 1911 with a group of eighteen new orchardists. In his study of Settlement Abandonment, Nelson Riis states that the Rhodes family sent young Rhodes to Walhachin as a disciplinary measure after he had been involved in inciting a riot in Costa Rica.

And all the English settlers, from the "select" group and also from the lower-born group, looked down on the non-English residents of the orchard community — the families of the CPR personnel, the employees of the cattle ranch, the employees of the poultry farm and the workers at "Angelsey."

Another factor which contributed to this unfortunate class distinction within the settlement was the fact that some of the titled landholders never came to Canada to "work" their orchard holdings at all. They paid the taxes, bought the land and financed the planting of the seedling trees, but they sent representatives to British Columbia to run their orchard properties — representatives who were decidedly not as well born as the landlords themselves.

This internal class distinction was one of the few things about the orchard enterprise which the residents, particularly the younger ones, regretted. They felt a genuine embarrassment because this situation had been allowed to become so firmly entrenched. But despite this class consciousness inside the community and the fact that the community stood aloof from the people of the surrounding areas, it certainly did not stand aloof from its links with England. During the summer months, the population almost doubled with the scores of visitors from home. And copies of letters sent to sons at Walhachin reveal a depth of affection and a sincere interest in the welfare of those absent family members which contradicts the suggestion that the families in question had welcomed a chance to send their unproductive members to Canada.

In any case, no matter what criticisms might be leveled against the orchardists as far as their upper-class social conscience is concerned, they cannot be faulted for their achievements. Considering their inexperience and their complete lack of skills, they accomplished an astonishing amount in the space of a few years. The Walhachin Hotel, for instance, was reputed to be the most luxurious and comfortable stopping place in the area. The homes of the individual residents were more modern and more comfortable than anything Ashcroft or Savona could boast. And the community hall was a truly outstanding piece of construction.

The decision to build the hall had been made in November, 1911, when it was evident that the hotel could no longer accomodate the number of people who wanted to attend dances, meetings and concerts. A committee was struck and plans were drawn. It was decided to purchase four lots to allow room for the construction of a sports complex which would surround the hall and include an ice rink for skating and curling, a grassed area for lawn bowling and additional tennis courts. It was decided that a series of card evenings and dances would be held

to raise immediate funds to start construction of the building, but that the bulk of the money would come from the sale of shares in the hall to the orchardists themselves.

Plans were drawn for a building some seventy-five feet in length with a main ballroom large enough to accomodate comfortably several hundred dancers. At the end of the room a large stage was erected, with a proscenium arch and space for hanging sets and backdrops for plays, concerts and other entertainments. Behind the stage on one side, a kitchen was built which included a cookstove for preparing refreshments; on the other side were cloakrooms and lavatory facilities for both ladies and gentlemen.

The floor of the hall, made of spruce planking, was constructed over underlying supports in such a way that there

Potatoes, grown as filler crops, provided a ready source of income.

Walhachin onions, grown between rows of seedling trees, were of exceptional quality.

was air space under the planking which allowed the floor to "float." Even today this floor is reputed to be the finest dancing floor in British Columbia.

Perhaps the most remarkable thing about the community hall was the heating and lighting system. A large steam furnace was installed in the basement, which worked on the same principle as a steam engine. At the bottom of the furnace there was a large compartment for wood and coal. Directly above this was the water compartment carefully marked with the maximum water line. From the top of the furnace pipes rose to carry the steam into the radiators which stood along the wall of the dance floor. Beside these pipes was a metal bellows with a gage attached. When the steam in the furnace expanded the bellows to a certain point, the gage automatically released some of the steam to relieve the build-up of pressure in the furnace. One of the early residents recalls having been assigned the task of emptying the furnace boiler about four o'clock in the morning after winter dances or concerts for if the water was allowed to stay in the furnace once the fire had been allowed to go out, it would freeze in the sub-zero temperatures.

The lights in the hall were the same carbide-pressure lamps that had been installed in all the private residences. Along the length of the ceiling a small pipe still remains into which, at regular intervals, the carbide lamps were fixed.

Some chroniclers have accused the orchardists of having been uncooperative and unwilling to work, but the evidence does not bear out this accusation. Most of the mistakes they made were the result of inexperience and stubbornness, not lack of effort. The filler crops of tomatoes, potatoes and onions planted between the rows of seedling apple trees to help defray expenses until the fruit trees should have matured, gained a reputation all across western Canada for excellence. In 1910, 1911 and 1912, record crops of these three products were marketed. And several of the orchardists branched into sidelines. Thomas Edwards (who later became manager of the general store) took up breeding chickens and game birds, and in January, 1912, he won prizes both in Calgary and in Revelstoke for his White Orpington Pullets and Cockerals.

Nor was interest in political issues forgotten. In January, 1911, a meeting was called at the hotel and there was unanimous agreement to form a Conservative Association, since in the words of the newly-elected executive, "it is important that newcomers should take an interest in the politics of their new homeland." Political debates were held among the orchardists and political speakers were invited to come to the community from other centres.

And it wasn't only the male members of the settlement who displayed initiative. Miss Netta Ricketts, who came from England in March, 1911, started a children's school within a month of her arrival. She had only five children to start, but enthusiasm made up for lack of numbers, and it was only the unreasonably hot weather in August that convinced Miss Ricketts to close the school for several weeks of summer vacation.

On September 2, 1911, the first edition of the *Walhachin Chronicle* was published. News items headed *Walhachin Chronicle* had been regularly appeared in the *Ashcroft Journal* since the previous May, but this was the first time a separate edition of the paper had been published. It was a single sheet, ten by fifteen inches, printed on both sides. In addition to the local Walhachin news, it included a detailed *London Letter* containing a report of the activities of the British Parliament, news of British union strikes, details of the first English Channel swim and a detailed story about the death of popular British novelist Katherine Temple Thurston. There was also a section which gave market reports, and an editorial. In one edition, this editorial commended the way residents of the orchard area invariably found a way to satisfy each new need that arose in their community. And the editor suggested the next project which should be considered was the establishment of a bank. The editorial two weeks later supported efforts to collect subscriptions toward the building of a church.

Only three editions of the *Walhachin Chronicle* were published as separate newspapers, but the *Chronicle* continued to be published as a part of the *Ashcroft Journal* for another five months. However, after the end of January, 1912, news items concerning Walhachin were run just as a part of the *Ashcroft Journal*, perhaps because the editor at Walhachin had found himself busy with other things.

On March 21, 1912, the first and only edition of the *Walhachin Times* was published. It too, was ten by fifteen inches in size, but while the *Chronicle* was one single sheet printed on both sides, the *Walhachin Times* was four pages. In its choice of news — predominantly British — and in its editorial tone, the Times was definitely "upper-class." A column headed "Sporting Notes by Our Bill," stated:

". . . Walhachin, for its size and population is one of the most sporting villages in this country or any other." There followed a plea for the grooming of a "few well-laid out holes for the enthusiastic golfers of the settlement" — a discussion of the relative inexpense of outfitting players for polo, if it were properly done — a brief mention of the success of the billiard tournament and an expression that another should be held as soon as possible — and then the column concluded with this remarkably provocative statement:

"There is rumor of a boxing show to be held in the town hall in March, and some talk of drawing a color line. . . . There is much to be said in favor of this." One must assume that "Our Bill" was worried about the boxing prowess of the Chinese field hands in the settlement, or perhaps of some of the ranchhands who might have been part Indian. But then, in an effort to assuage the feelings of any of his more equality conscious readers, Our Bill conceded that perhaps one should admit, "at

Oxford and Cambridge no such line has ever been drawn."

But what the *Walhachin Times* obviously lacked in human-rights consciousness, it made up for in local pride. The editorial of this single edition of the paper states complacently (if in places, ungrammatically):

"Much hot air has been expended upon Walhachin as a fruit proposition, rightly or wrongly, but little time or attention has been paid it from a residential point of view.

"Walhachin today as a residential proposition would be hard to beat, and requires no real estate agents to promote it. . . . Where in the whole of British Columbia could you find such a superb climate, view or comfort? . . . The residential part lies in a hollow, sheltered by mountains all around, with the magnificent Thompson River running below the townsite. There are good driving roads all around, and now that the Government bridge has been completed, easy access is afforded to the surrounding country."

One wonders if perhaps the *modus vivendi* behind this second newspaper had been to oppose the views of the editor of the *Walhachin Chronicle*, who had pleaded so eloquently for the cause of a church in the settlement, for after his words of praise the *Times* editor continues:

"Does Walhachin require a church? Can Walhachin afford a church? I venture to say that Walhachin now having a town hall, which has been erected at considerable self-sacrifice to those who have generously taken shares, does not need a church."

Perhaps the most significant indication of the way the original orchard settlers demonstrated their involvement in the welfare of their new community was in the burgeoning number and diversity of businesses which these enterprising Englishmen developed within a year or two of their arrival.

The first business established was the general store which opened in early 1910. Then in July of that year, the Walhachin Poultry Ranch was established at the eastern end of the townsite. Within twelve months, it had expanded to house more than a hundred birds.

In August, 1910, N.E. Gore-Langton opened his Bait and Livery Stable. Earlier that summer Captain Peebles had established the 5PX Livery Stable and had purchased a string of livery horses. This venture proved profitable and in July, 1911, Peebles sold his business to C.T. Gardner, and opened the 5 PX Laundry instead.

In May, 1911, a butcher shop was opened with Gordon Flowerdew in charge. The butcher shop was operated in conjunction with the general store. Now for the first time the residents of the orchard settlement could buy fresh meat without having to go to Ashcroft or Savona, an all-day buggy trip.

In July, 1911, the Walhachin Restaurant was opened. That same month Mrs. Hamilton-Warde delighted the other residents by opening a bakery. According to the Ashcroft Journal, ". . . the oven, constructed on modern lines, is supplying all the bread to the hotel and to the restaurant, as well as to the private homes. Cakes and buns are made to order on request."

That same summer, Miss Ricketts, who had opened the first school in March, 1911, branched into a Ladies' Haberdashery Store. It was advertised as being open for business from eight to nine o'clock each morning and from three to five o'clock each afternoon, so it would not interfere with her school teaching. In the fall, she also opened a Gentlemen's Haberdashery Store.

By the fall of 1911 the 5PX Stables, which C.T. Gardner now owned, had expanded its business to include potato hauling, an extremely profitable operation. That fall an estimated 2,000 tons of Walhachin potatoes raised as filler crops were transported to market. Also that fall, two building companies were established, one managed by the Honorable H.M. Nelson-Hood and the other by M.W. Hemming. W.H. Snell opened an Insurance and Real Estate Office and a second restaurant started business. In November, the 5PX Stables again expanded with the purchase of a herd of dairy cows and now for the first time fresh milk was available right in the settlement.

In December, 1911, Mrs. Hamilton-Warde expanded her bakery to include another restaurant and in January, 1912, Miss Ricketts added a Drapery and Millinery Shop to her other business interests. At the same time Captain Peebles moved into chicken farming and built a large poultry shed which housed more than a hundred birds.

The residents of Walhachin even managed to provide their own law enforcement officers. W.H. Snell, manager of the thriving Insurance and Real Estate Office, had been a successful lawyer before leaving England to come to Walhachin. In January, 1911, he was appointed Justice of the Peace. And when in October of that year a store owned by some of the Chinese laborers was broken into, two orchardists, Gordon Flowerdew and A.K. Loyd, were sworn in as special deputies and sent to apprehend the thief. They did so with dispatch.

There was little need, however, for law enforcement within the settlement itself for it was a closely knit community. But unfortunately, there were times when the English settlement as a

59

whole was in legal trouble with its neighbors. On two different occasions lawsuits were launched against the orchard community: once, when the British Columbia Horticultural Estates Company violated a water rights agreement,[1] and the second time when a workman was refused admission to the beverage room in the Walhachin Hotel. In fact, the *Ashcroft Journal*'s yearly reports on the large numbers of Walhachin residents who were in attendance at each annual meeting of the Clinton Assizes, suggests that there may have been more occasions than just these two when the orchardists could have been at odds with their neighbors.

Meanwhile, it was inevitable that during the time the orchardists were expending every effort to enlarge their business interests and to develop their community, a number of Canadians moved in among the English residents. And if the orchardists were resourceful and innovative, so were the Canadians, particularly Alphonse and Fanny Faucault.

It was Fanny who was the chief pianist at the balls and concerts — whose house was always open to receive the "strays" and the unexpected arrivals who came to the settlement. And although some chroniclers credit the Marquis of Angelsey with being the driving force behind the acquisition of the famed "Paderewski piano," it was more Fanny Faucault's doing. She was the person who had originally encouraged the orchardists to buy a grand piano for their newly completed community hall, rather than an upright. And she advised a delegation to go from Walhachin to Vancouver to look for a suitable instrument. The group located a Webber concert grand that Paderewski had used during his North American tour and had left in Vancouver when he returned to Europe. The group bought the piano for a reasonable sum and took it back to the orchard community to be put in the hall. Fanny Faucault then proceeded to organize a small orchestra which hired itself out to play for dances, and donated all its earnings toward the mortgage on the hall.

Al Faucault, a mule-team driver, had earned a reputation on the Cariboo Road for accepting all the jobs the other drivers considered dangerous. The story is told by Harry Taylor in the *Kamloops Sentinel* of an occasion in the days before there was a bridge across the river at Walhachin. An appeal had been made for someone to carry a message across to Ashcroft, but the river was too swollen with spring rains for the ferry to run. ". . . The only one who stepped forward was Alphonse Faucault. Despite a chorus of protests against what looked like sure suicide, he rode the flood waters on a telegraph pole."

On another occasion Taylor recounted a story Fanny told about her husband. Apparently, early one morning in the spring of 1910, Archie Styer, who had been empowered to act as estate manager at Walhachin during one of Charles Barnes' short absences occasioned by a visit to England, awoke Faucault to ask his assistance in delivering the body of a dead Chinese laborer to the police constable in Ashcroft. "The roads were a muddy mess, and no horses were available," Taylor writes. "The only car was a new Ford belonging to the absent Barnes, and neither Archie Styer nor Al Faucault knew how to drive." They constructed a coffin for the dead man then, despite their lack of driving expertise, they put the body into the back of the Ford and set out. But apparently the mud road was practically impassable. At the top of one particularly steep hill they realized there was no way they could hope to keep the car on the road all the way to the bottom. So, Taylor writes, "Al Faucault got out and tied himself behind the car. And with him as both brake and rudder, Styer managed to side-slip the Ford down the greasy hill and safely into Ashcroft."

Obviously, the Canadians at Walhachin, though middle-class and few in number, could match their English fellows as far as spunk and ingenuity were concerned.

Footnotes:

[1] Nelson A. Riis, "Settlement Abandonment — A Case Study of Walhachin." Unpublished Master's Thesis, Department of Geography, University of British Columbia, 1970.

61

The Women

Inside the Bennie house at Walhachin.

For the female members of the community, life at Walhachin was far from easy, particularly when most of them were accustomed to leisured, upper-class lives in England. And although some women brought domestic servants with them, their lifestyle in the orchard settlement was one of active involvement rather than leisured dependency.

It must have been a severe shock to most of them having travelled 6,000 miles, to discover the isolation of their new community. Undoubtedly they were unprepared for the extremes of temperature between winter readings of twenty-five and thirty degrees below zero Fahrenheit (thirty-two and thirty-five degrees below zero Celsius) and summer readings of over 100 degrees Fahrenehit (thirty-eight degrees Celsius) for days at a time. In addition, one can imagine their feelings at viewing the

Graceful living.

dry cactus-covered hills after they had just left the gently rolling green fields of England. Instead of primroses and wild roses, all Walhachin could offer was her indigenous cactus with its saucy yellow-pink blossoms. And the ubiquitous dust must have been a constant trial. But they had come to Canada to make their homes, bringing with them all their fine china, silver and chippendale furniture — wearing their ball gowns, furs and jewelry — and they had no option but to make the best of things. So make the best of things they did.

Many of the women, like Miss Ricketts and Mrs. Hamilton-Warde, branched out into business ventures along side of the men. Others provided the impetus for a good part of the community's hospitality, and initiated plans for most of its entertainments. And almost all of them undertook — perhaps

Yearling trees on B.C. Horticultural Estates Company, Walhachin.

not eagerly, but certainly not begrudgingly — to fulfill whatever duties and responsibilities this new life should thrust in their way.

Among the possessions of one of the wives was a notebook, dated 1911, which contained this piece of information in the middle of its recipes:

"About hens and ducks: — Hens hatched in February will begin to lay in November when they are nine months old, so you must hatch chickens according to the time you want them to lay. Hens will not lay in the winter after the first year, so it is better to kill them off after that, as they are only eating a lot of food and will only produce eggs in the summer. Ducks more than a year old will only lay in the spring."

A little farther along in the same notebook was the following item:

"Swellings and sprains: — equal parts of metholated spirits of water if the skin is not broken. If it is, then use a fourth of the spirit with water. Bathe with this."

Nor were the women inclined to be lazy when it came to fulfilling their duties as housekeepers. Few modern women would relish following this hand written recipe:

"To cure hams — for each sixteen pound ham take four ounces of bay salt and two ounces of salt petre and pound it well. Add one ounce of black pepper and one pound of brown sugar. Rub this mixture well into each ham. Allow hams to lie for four days. Then put half a pound of treacle over each one, and let them lie in the treacle for one month. At the end of this month wash the hams and hang them to dry, then wrap them in paper. Soak for twelve to twenty-four hours before boiling them."

But if, on the one hand, the women had to adjust to frontier living and to assume duties and responsibilities that most of them would never have dreamed of having to tackle at home in England, on the other, they had no intention of sacrificing the qualities of life that they felt were important. Proper manners, dress, and social behavior were still their prime concern. Perhaps they had moved 6,000 miles away from the society they loved, but that move was no excuse for being unfashionable. The ball gowns worn to the parties at the hotel or the community hall were of the most modern design, and they were accompanied by fur capes and long white evening gloves. And even for dinner in their own homes, most of the wives invariably changed into evening clothes. They kept in touch with the fashions at home, and English magazines dated 1911, 1912 and 1913 displaying the latest styles in skirts and dresses were sent from England.

One early resident had made special note of information advising the modern young lady on the proper equestrian etiquette, perhaps with a view to taking part in one of the fox hunts. The clipping she had saved, dated November, 1913, advised the reader, "Now-a-days many girls ride astride, though many still prefer the side saddle. In either case a short corset is better than a long one, but above all, a comfortable one should be selected. The hair should be dressed in an exceedingly simple fashion. Artificial hair should be abandoned, and the locks braided and tied neatly with a bow of black ribbon at the nape of the neck. Leave combs, shell hairpins and hatpins at home. The latter are exceedingly dangerous and many bad accidents have occurred by reason of their being jammed into the head, or by the hat flying off causing the pin to strike one of the other members of the party.

"For the rest of the costume, a shirt waist with a well-fitting stock always looks smart. Leather gloves a size larger than usual should be worn, and a long riding skirt or a separated skirt, depending on the choice of saddle."

But the increased capabilities and accomplishments that the women of Walhachin were displaying did nothing to change the opinions of the men in the settlement as to the role of the female sex. In December, 1910, a debate was held in the hotel on the subject: "Resolved, that the suffrage should be given to women". The affirmative side of the argument was proposed by John Bertram, whose wife had presented the settlement with its first baby, a son, some few days previously, and by B.C. Footner, recently returned from England with his new bride. The negative side was upheld by J. Billinghurst and William Higgs, both of whom were bachelors. When a vote was taken at the conclusion of the debate, seventy-five per cent of those present voted decisively against the resolution. It is open to conjecture how many of the remaining twenty-five per cent were women.

However, there were distinct advantages to be gained from allowing the men to enjoy their feeling of supremacy. The women were treated with every courtesy and consideration. At the dances, it was unheard of for any woman to be left standing on the sidelines, and the arrival of a new woman in the settlement was greeted with excitement. In fact, a ticket to Walhachin almost insured one of finding a husband. Freda Kendall came to the orchard settlement to help her sister, Mrs. H. M. Nelson-Hood, to take care of a newborn baby. But before the baby was safely over its first three months, Miss Kendall was married and ready to start thinking about a family of her own.

However it must be admitted that even matrimony was not sufficient inducement to persuade some of the wellborn English misses to stay in the rural settlement. In August, 1910, builder Footner completed a new house, for the two newly-arrived Misses Wortley-Watson. By September, one was engaged to be married and the other had booked passage to return to England.

The unnatural imbalance between the large number of single men in the settlement and the relative scarcity of single women resulted in many orchardists taking advantage of the winter months to return to England for a bride. The arrival of each newly-married lady received mention in the columns of the *Ashcroft Journal*. Even the prospect of an impending engagement was considered sufficiently important to be given public notice, though it was not always treated perfectly seriously. In January, 1912, the *Journal* ran an item about an orchardist named Snell, who had arrived in Walhachin with the first group of settlers. Snell was by then the manager of a thriving Insurance and Real Estate office, Justice of the Peace for Walhachin and active in the Walhachin Conservative party. But apparently during all his months in Walhachin he had studiously avoided getting involved in any of the social activities, or at least he had until that time. It is with amusement that the *Ashcroft Journal* in January, 1912, states, "Mr. Wm. H. Snell, the hermit of Walhachin, has finally budded out. Every evening now bridge games and musical gatherings take place in his cosy rooms. And we hope that once again Cupid's rumors will prove to be correct."

The standards of dress and behavior which the women of Walhachin set for themselves were maintained for the children in the settlement as well. The number of children in Walhachin was never large. It totalled only eleven in 1910, five of school age and the remainder teen-agers, and though a number of births were recorded in the following years, the number of children never swelled to more than twenty. But for the few who were there, the orchardists maintained a strict well-disciplined life-style.

From the time that Netta Ricketts arrived in March, 1911, there was always a school in the settlement. When the number of school-age youngsters fell below the ten required by the Provincial Department of Education to justify the provision of a government-financed school and a government-salaried teacher, the orchardists provided the necessary funds out of their own pockets, and the teacher was boarded at the home of one of the pupils. And the high standard of teaching is evident from the number of children from outlying areas who could have chosen to attend schools in Ashcroft or Savona, but who chose instead to come to Walhachin. In fact, in some instances parents of pupils paid for their children to board with one of the orchard families during the course of an entire school year.

The school was housed in a number of different buildings — sometimes in a private home, sometimes in an unused office — and even at one time in the store building. But the quality of the instruction never varied.

The work was divided into first, second and third Primer, and first, second, third and fourth Reader. The subjects taught included arithmetic, grammar, geography, history (both Canadian and British) nature study, dictation and spelling, English literature, drawing and writing. Prizes were given each year in each of these areas, as well as for deportment and for written homework. And an "Honor Roll" for proficiency in any subject was a coveted prize.

In the opinion of many of the pupils who attended the one-room school at Walhachin, it had many advantages. Perhaps the greatest was the value of repetition. As each child worked at his own level, he could not help overhearing the lessons being taught to the others. And since the teacher, faced with the problem of keeping seven programs running con-currently, tended to concentrate on basics, it was these necessary foundation stones that the children heard repeated year after year. Even the slowest pupil was sure to have absorbed most of them by the time he graduated from the fourth Reader.

Another advantage resulted from the mixing of different ages and sizes of pupils. A tolerance for smaller children and a respect for older and stronger ones — two qualities that are often lacking in children whose associations have been strictly limited to children of the same age and size — were unconsciously developed.

Certainly the number of children was small, and the settlement was relatively isolated, but in spite of this the young people enjoyed a happy, well-structured lifestyle. As soon as they were old enough and sufficiently skillful, they were welcomed into the sporting events which formed such a large part of the activities of the adult population. They were included in the cultural evenings and often took part in the concerts. And, though they did not attend the balls, on the morning after each one the children stopped by to claim their share of the leftover treats. Many had their own horses to ride, and the irrigation ditches running from Brassey Creek and Jimmie Creek, which provided water for the townsite, were alive with trout. On their way home from school in the afternoons the boys filled their lunch pails with fish.

A favorite event for the girls was the election each year of a May Queen. The winning of this honor was considered the highlight of the year.

At Christmas and Hallowe'en, and on other special occasions, Manager Barnes and his wife organized parties. With no children of their own, they delighted in planning parties for the children of the orchard residents.

And the dense beaver population on the north shore, which caused such problems with the irrigation ditches that weekly patrols had to be organized to insure that newly-built beaver dams should not stop the flow of water, was a source of delight to the young boys of Walhachin. According to one early resident, they considered the weekly patrols to look for beaver dams to be "tremendous treats".

The Seeds of Failure

Potatoes growing as a filler crop between the apple trees.

The orchard enterprise at Walhachin appeared to be flourishing. The orchardists had succeeded in reclaiming the desert fields and in constructing an irrigation system to service them. They had succeeded in establishing a diversity of business enterprises. They had succeeded in establishing a commendable level of education for their children. Most important of all, they had succeeded in establishing a life style to match the one they had left in England, where sporting interests were paramount and where social and cultural activities were legion.

The accusation has been made that the orchardists were more interested in enjoying themselves than in working to make their holdings prosper. No doubt this is true, but it must be acknowledged that in spite of their preference for sport and leisured living, these Englishmen accomplished a surprising

amount in the few years that they peopled the orchard settlement.

It had been in the fall of 1909 that the first section of orchard had been cleared and planted. That had been the area previously occupied by the Pennie ranch, and cultivation of it had been easy for it was already free of rocks and sage brush. Before winter set in that first year, fifty acres had been planted with seedling trees.

The following spring work began on the remaining 250 acres of arable land adjacent to the townsite on the south shore of the river. During the spring and the summer the entire 250 acres was cultivated, and an estimated 36,000 seedling trees were planted. This completed the available amount of arable acreage on the south shore.

In 1911 Barnes and the orchardists began work on the north

bank of the river. Now the British Columbia Horticultural Estates Company purchased two new steam tractors and the business of clearing the land progressed at a much faster rate. During 1911, 1912 and 1913 a total of almost 1,000 acres of land was cleared and seeded, bringing the total acreage under cultivation on both sides of the river to just over 1,240 acres.

This was a notable achievement. According to reports in the *Ashcroft Journal*, some 44,000 seedlings were set out. The varieties of apples planted included Jonathons, Wealthies, Wagoners, Spitzenbergs and Rome Beauties, but in the earliest sections cultivated, Jonathons and Wagoners were preferred, for while all other brands require five to six years to mature, Jonathons and Wagoners produce fruit in only four years.

In addition to apples the orchardists also planted a small

Inspecting a nearly mature tree.

Steam tractors lined up ready for work in the fields.

number of other fruit trees — pears, peaches, apricots, plums and cherries. And, of course, between the rows they planted their intermediate crops of potatoes, tomatoes and onions.

Returns were realized immediately on the intermediate crops. In the fall of 1910 more than 2,000 tons of Walhachin potatoes were shipped to market and by the following year the settlement had established a name for itself for producing fine tomatoes and onions.

In the fall of 1912 the first apples were beginning to appear on trees planted in 1909. And in 1913, as reported in both the *Ashcroft Journal* and the *Inland Sentinel*, a large shipment of apples went from Walhachin to centres all across Canada.

In the spring of 1914 it was evident from the blossoms on 600 acres of Jonathons and Wagoners that the settlement could

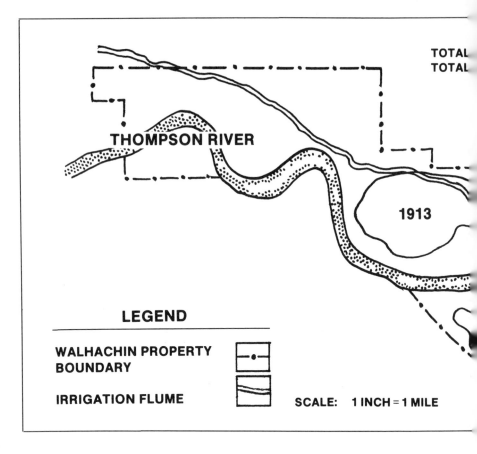

TOTAL
TOTAL

THOMPSON RIVER

1913

LEGEND

WALHACHIN PROPERTY
BOUNDARY

IRRIGATION FLUME

SCALE: 1 INCH = 1 MILE

expect a record crop that fall. And the orchardists were not disappointed. In October, a full "trainload of apples", in the terms of the October 31, 1914, edition of the *Ashcroft Journal*, "of exceptionally high quality", were harvested and shipped to markets across Canada. But, unfortunately, only a few of the original orchardists were present to enjoy this achievement, for almost all the men of military age had left the settlement in August, either with the Walhachin Company of the 31st British Columbia Horse, or to rejoin their old regiments in England, and many of their wives had gone with them.

Many chroniclers claim that this mass exodus after the outbreak of war was what brought about the failure of the orchard settlement. But even if war had not intervened, it is doubtful if the orchard project would have survived, or if it could

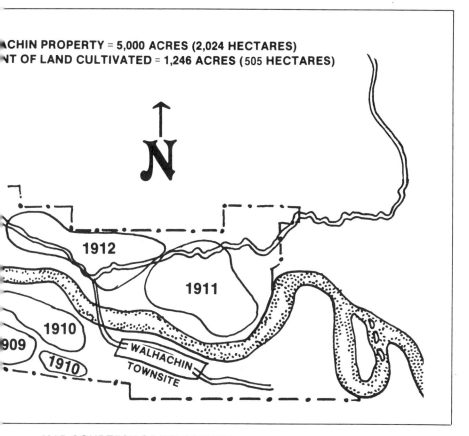

ACHIN PROPERTY = 5,000 ACRES (2,024 HECTARES)
NT OF LAND CULTIVATED = 1,246 ACRES (505 HECTARES)

N

1912

1911

1910

909

1910

WALHACHIN
TOWNSITE

MAP COURTESY OF NELSON RIIS

ever have proven to be a success financially. For though the orchardists themselves did not seem to realize it, the seeds of failure had been present since the beginning.

An important factor to be considered was the amount of acreage under cultivation. True, the clearing and seeding of 1,246 acres of land in the course of four growing seasons had been a notable achievement. And it is open to conjecture, whether or not had that progress continued, the future of the settlement would have been any different. But that progress did not continue, and not because of the war. That progress did not continue because the 1,246 acres that had been seeded represented the only land in the entire 5,000 acres of Walhachin property that was suitable for cultivation. The rest was unsuitable either because of the nature of the soil itself, or

75

because it was of inadequate depth over a rock base.

But even if two or three times as much acreage had been cultivated it is still doubtful if the project could have succeeded, for the major factor leading to failure was inescapable. It was inescapable because it lay within the character of the orchardists themselves. Paradoxically, those very strengths which enabled them to create their "ideal" society in the midst of the wilderness, to build an orchard in a virtual desert and to make that orchard bear fruit — those typically English upper-class qualities of pride, determination, self-reliance, a supreme confidence in their own capabilities and a feeling of tolerant condescension toward the abilities of everyone else — were the very qualities which brought about the settlement's eventual failure.

It was inconceivable to the orchardists that any advice or information that a "colonial" might have to offer, could be of any real value. In addition, it was considered "infra dig" for an Englishman to defer to the opinion of an obvious social inferior. Consequently, the orchardists made no attempt to attend any local meetings or to consult with any of the surrounding residents concerning problems in the orchards. The residents of Walhachin maintained the same aloofness in professional matters that they did in social ones.

However, it should be conceded here that there was another side to the situation. While the orchardists were unwilling to put themselves into the position of asking advice of their neighbors, the local residents made every effort to avoid offering any.

One wonders if the hard-working residents of the surrounding centres might not have enjoyed seeing the sports-loving, pleasure-seeking Englishmen making their blunders — they might not even have been hoping to see the eventual failure of the orchard settlement. Certainly, they felt dislike for and resentment of the residents of "little England."

The fact that the orchardists only mixed with the local residents at sporting events, and then beat the local teams with embarrassing regularity undoubtedly added to this and may well have been a major factor behind the encouragement on the part of the surrounding centres of the formation of Walhachin hockey and curling teams — neither of which performed successfully.

Undeniably, the residents of the outlying centres resented the haughty upper-class standards set in the Walhachin Hotel beverage rooms. The fact that the refusal to admit a local workman had been sufficient provocation for a lawsuit is proof of this. And, though the result of that lawsuit ended segregation in the hotel, few residents of Savona or Ashcroft ever patronized the Walhachin Hotel for dinner or for afternoon tea.

A glimpse at the lifestyle enjoyed by the orchard wives must also have incurred jealousy. Not only did the women of Walhachin own houses complete with every possible comfort, but they were furnished with beautiful furniture, fine English bone china and Irish linens. And the elaborate balls and parties held at Walhachin were closed to neighboring families. The only outside guests allowed to attend were socially acceptable individuals who had some personal association with the titled members of the orchard community. And even if the ordinary people of the surrounding towns had been invited, they could not have accepted, for they would have possessed nothing sufficiently stylish or formal to wear.

So, on the one hand, while the orchardists made no effort to seek the expertise of their neighbors, on the other, if such overtures had been made they would probably have been soundly rebuffed. As a result, Walhachin was unrepresented at local meetings or gatherings called for the purpose of advancing the business of orchard development.

In 1919 national interest in fruit production was high. Meetings, lectures and study sessions were common. In February the British Columbia Fruit Growers Association called a reorganizational meeting. The membership fee was set at only one dollar, and the association anticipated a minimum of 1,000 potential members to attend. Only ninety-seven turned up, and of those ninety-seven not a single representative came from Walhachin.

That same spring another meeting was called, to which came farmers and fruit growers from all over the British Columbia Interior. The purpose of the meeting was to discuss the control of damage to crops. The meeting was considering asking the government to increase the present bounties of five dollars a head on coyotes, and of three cents a head on gophers and moles in order to reduce the amount of damage they caused. In the words of the meeting, ". . . particularly the gophers and moles were most destructive, eating away at the roots of the seedling trees during the winter." But the well-attended meeting finally decided not to pursue the question, for it was decided that ". . . the problem was not serious on the bottom lands, but was only of real concern on the benches." The benches, of course, referred to just such lands as those the Walhachin orchardists were cultivating. If a single representative from Walhachin had been in attendance at that meeting, perhaps a great deal of

subsequent reseeding might have been avoided.

The orchardists of Walhachin were also noticeably absent from later meetings when fruit farmers in the area were instructed in the use of proper "washes" of lime sulphate or copper sulphate with which the trees should have been coated in the fall in order to prevent winter damage. Nor did they attend instructional meetings advising orchardists to clear all vegetation from between the rows of fruit trees during the winter months, for it was a natural breeding ground for mice and rabbits, both of which would happily spend the winter nibbling at the trees. But instead of clearing the area between their rows of trees, the orchardists at Walhachin followed the advice of the promoters and planted intermediate crops of potatoes, onions and tomatoes in these areas, and in the fall, rather than stripping

The packing house at Walhachin.

1910 Barnes Estates.

away all the leaves and decaying vegetation, they mistakenly left it where it was as additional fertilizer.

Some people have accused the orchardists of making no effort to educate themselves, but this accusation is not entirely justified. True, they showed a reluctance to ask advice of their neighbors, and they failed to attend the meetings of the fruit industry. Admittedly, the horticultural school advertised in the Walhachin brochure never materialized. And it is also true that only two Walhachin orchardists elected to take advantage of the excellent training courses offered during the off-season at the Pullman Technical College in Pullman, Washington,[1] and that those two orchardists were the only ones who made a good profit out of their orchard land. But at the same time, it is not true that the orchardists as a group made no effort to educate themselves. During the first three or four years when the orchards were being planted, guest horticulturalists were invited regularly to address the settlers.

In August, 1910, Thomas Cunningham, the Provincial Fruit Inspector, was invited to come to the settlement. According to the report in the *Ashcroft Journal*, "over 44,000 trees had been planted at that time, the largest single planting in Canada. Mr. Cunningham reported that he found the orchard in absolutely clean condition, in fact that it is the cleanest orchard he has ever inspected."

In July, 1911, Professor Thatcher, the director of the Experimental Station at Pullman, Washington, was invited to Walhachin to address the orchardists on the business side of fruit farming. And that fall, as a result of some lobbying on the part of the Walhachin settlers, the government fruit inspector came to Walhachin to present a practical demonstration of orchard work, the first of its kind ever given.[2]

The problem did not lie in whether or not the orchardists took suitable steps to learn the business of fruit farming. The problem lay in the fact that they neglected to ask professional advice in those areas where mistakes could not be rectified, and where their customary methods of learning through trial and error could not be employed.

It was arrogance and misplaced self-confidence which precluded their asking for advice concerning the design and the construction of the flume and the irrigation ditches. Their failure to build the flume structure in separate sections, or to line the irrigation ditches with gravel, was critical. So was their failure to purchase suitable lumber or to caulk the boards properly. In his study of Settlement Abandonment Nelson Riis states: "Proper flumes require two-inch thick boards, caulked by placing oiled rope between the planks. At Walhachin the flume joints were caulked with oakum only where the flume circumvented a bluff, and only a very few sections in the length of the whole structure received tar applications."[3]

This same propensity for recklessly pushing ahead without stopping to ask advice of anyone resulted in the orchardists planting insufficiently hardy varieties of apples in certain un-protected areas, and in their wasting both money and effort planting soft fruits such as pears and peaches, neither of which could survive the Walhachin winters.

Their stubborn independence led them to persist in planting varieties of vegetables and berries in their gardens which were totally unsuited to either the soil or the weather conditions. And the fact that a fellow orchardist had already tried a certain species and proved it to be unsuitable meant nothing — each orchardist had to see for himself. If he had grown such things at home in England, he was determined to grow the same things in Walhachin. Advice from anyone, even from members of their own community, was seldom invited.

But it must be admitted that on those few occasions when the orchardists did ask for advice, what was offered was far from helpful. In fact, it seemed that the English orchardists were cursed with an abundance of misleading advice and inaccurate information. The initial surveys done by agriculturalist Palmer and engineer Ashcroft from Lord Aberdeen's estates, were certainly incomplete and indirectly misleading. If either man had been proficient in his area of work he could not have helped but recognize the impracticality of irrigating fields which lay 1,100 feet above the level of the river — he could not have helped but notice that large areas of the fields in question contained only a thin layer of soil over an impenetrable rock base which rendered tree planting impossible.

The soil surveys of the Walhachin acreage were equally misleading.[4] They suggested that the soil throughout the entire 5,000 acres was of uniform quality and "would grow a wide variety of produce provided it received sufficient moisture." However, when the orchardists arrived to take possession of their land, they discovered that every ten-acre holding included large patches of unarable land. In the case of some of the orchardists, the unarable portion was greater than fifty per cent of the holding.

Surely any resident of a neighboring community could have told Palmer, Ashcroft or Barnes that the climate on the Thompson River benchlands was not suited to fruit production of any kind. Anyone who had lived there for more than a few years must have known that the winter temperature lows of thirty degrees below zero Fahrenheit (thirty-five degrees Celsius) accompanied by freezing winds were not conducive to fruit growing, nor were the blazing hot months of summer when the lack of moisture combined with the reflection of the heat off the baked clay soil scalded the fruit before it was ready for picking. But seemingly, no one did. This information appeared in none of the early studies.

In retrospect, it seems incredible that even the agricultural experts of the day asked no questions and paid scant attention to past weather records. Early in 1910 the first group of orchardists decided to plant tobacco as one of their intermediate crops. With the long hot summer it did extremely well. In November the orchardists invited L. Holman, the provincial tobacco inspector in Kelowna, to come to Walhachin to inspect the crop. According to the *Ashcroft Journal*, Inspector Holman reported that the Walhachin crop "was in excellent condition," that he was "pleased with the leaf," and that the orchardists could expect "a bountiful harvest in January when the plants will be ready to strip." No one even considered the fact that by January the crop would have lain in the drying shed through two months of below freezing temperatures, which could not help but damage the leaves.

This same incomplete knowledge was apparent in the advice given the orchardists about their intermediate crops. Undoubtedly, the cultivation of these crops provided a source of income for the orchardists during those years while they waited for their apple trees to start to bear fruit, but the trees themselves would have fared better if the land between the rows had been left fallow.

As for the financial failure of the project, the blame cannot be placed entirely on the shoulders of the orchardists themselves. Certainly, their refusal to ask advice about the care of their orchards resulted in loss of seedlings and decrease in apple production in some areas. And their failure to attend meetings or to take courses certainly resulted in trial and error methods. But other factors, too, were involved in determining that the orchard settlement could never have proved financially viable.

In the first place it must be conceded that the attempt to build an orchard on the benchlands of the Thompson River was an impossible task from the outset. The necessity for the construction of an irrigation system which, even when it was built as hastily and with as inferior materials as was done at Walhachin, still cost in excess of $100,000, could not be absorbed by a total orchard acreage of only 1,246 acres. Even had the entire 5,000 acres proven arable, it is still doubtful if that amount of orchard could have provided sufficient revenue to repay the expense of the original irrigation system and to maintain its constantly needed repairs.

Another factor which contributed to the financial problems of the orchard settlement, though not realized until after fruit production was underway, was that the Canadian Pacific and Canadian National railways would only agree to carry fruit shipments on certain of their regular trains. Both railways had stations at Walhachin — a fact extolled in the original promotion brochure. The CPR ran three transcontinental trains through the settlement every day. It had even constructed a "Y" in the middle of the townsite where loaded cars could wait to be picked up. The grade of the roadbed from North Bend to Pennie Station was so steep that an engine could pull only thirty rail cars. But after Walhachin the grade was much less steep all the way to Craigellachie, a distance of over 220 miles. The "Y" at Walhachin station meant that a steam engine could bring up one loaded train, drop off the cars, return to North Bend for thirty more and then continue east with a full sixty-car load.

But daily trains and conveniently located "Y's" were of no value when only certain trains, which came at infrequent intervals, would accept fruit as part of their freight. The result was boxes of fruit, picked and ready for shipping, sitting in the scorching sun for hours and sometimes days at a time while train after train passed, until that one particular train which would accept fruit came along.

Another problem, perhaps one of the most serious, was that of the competition from the United States fruit producers. The more than 44,000 seedlings planted at Walhachin had all been purchased from nurseries in the United States, in spite of the fact that the newspapers of the day carried regular ads for fruit trees at nurseries in Vancouver. Perhaps this preference was the result of Charles Barnes' influence, or it may have been because the quantity of trees required and the particular varieties of apple wanted — specifically Jonathons and Wagoners — had made it necessary to buy them in the United States. But whatever the reason, the freight costs and the inevitable damage to some of the seedlings as a result of their being transported such a distance increased the initial seeding costs. In addition, expenses connected with the whole business of apple production were much higher in Canada than in the United States.

At the Annual Fruit Growers' Convention held in Vancouver in November, 1913, the matter received considerable attention. The meeting was informed that because of the length of the growing season and the general climate conditions, the average yield of apples per tree in the United States was noticeably higher than in Canada. In addition, American labor costs were lower, as was the American government tax rate on orchard land. Moreover, the price American fruit farmers paid for water was between twenty and thirty per cent lower than that paid in Canada and the cost of orchard machinery, paper and boxes for packing was between thirty and forty per cent lower. As a result, the meeting was informed, the total cost of production of fruit in the United States ran at a figure approximately thirty per cent below what British Columbia orchardists paid. In addition the Walhachin settlers had to pay an annual fee of four dollars per acre to the British Columbia Horticultural Estates Company as a surcharge to help defray the costs of the irrigation system. Yet in spite of this noticeable difference in production costs, American apples were allowed to come in to the country to compete with Canadian fruit. Certainly duty was charged, but it was only thirteen cents a box, which did not make up even a quarter of the difference.

There were problems too with actual marketing methods. The American orchardists with their larger volume of sales, were able to market what they termed a "fancy" grade apple at only a slightly higher price than the "regular" grade. These fancy apples still came into Canada at the same thirteen cent duty rate, and were guaranteed to sell, for not only were they of superior quality, but they were much less expensive than Canadian fruit with its thirty per cent higher production costs.

As a final straw, it seemed that the Canadian producer was also faced with unfair trade practices. In July, 1911, M.P. McNeill, the Dominion fruit inspector, publicly announced in Ottawa that the British Columbia fruit grower had no protection from American competition. He went on to say, that in addition to the problems of lower American production costs, and the ridiculously small import duties imposed by the Canadian government, that the American fruit industry was also guilty of using a smaller-sized box than the Canadian fruit producers used. Of course, the American quart box for berry fruits was only four-fifths of the imperial quart used in Canada, but Mr. McNeill went on to state, "American fruit boxes (used for apples and other tree fruits) although to all appearances of a standard size until placed along side of the British Columbia product, often have false bottoms." Whether or not this criticism was truly justified is open to debate, but the combination of all the other factors, added to the lack of experience of the Walhachin orchardists and their trial and error methods, made it not at all surprising that they found it impossible to compete as far as price was concerned with the American apples which flooded into Canada each fall. Nor could they anticipate any improvement in the situation. On the contrary, the cost of their production was inevitably going to increase as the poorly constructed flume required more and more extensive repairs. But in the years prior to World War I, the orchardists seemed unaware of this. Few of them had anticipated making any profit for at least six years after arriving in Walhachin. In fact the advertising brochure which the BCDA distributed set out detailed tables of figures which showed capital outlay, taxes and the returns the orchardists could expect from their intermediate crops, and stated very clearly that it would take a minimum of six years before the orchards would be sufficiently mature to realize sufficient revenue to repay each orchardist's investment. Accordingly, in those pre-war years the orchardists were undismayed by the small returns which were realized. In fact, the bonus of a small marketable crop in 1913 which no one had expected, followed by the promise of a record harvest the next fall, made it seem that their orchard enterprise was finally becoming profitable. And even the outbreak of war and the enlistment of a large number of men of military age did nothing to dispel this optimism. They had every expectation that the orchards would continue to prosper, and that the size of the harvest would continue to grow, for a number of older men still remained in the settlement to tend the fruit trees as did some of the hired laborers. Besides, they were sure that the war would last only six months at the very outside.

Footnotes:

[1] Nelson A. Riis, "Settlement Abandonment — A Case Study of Walhachin." Unpublished Master's Thesis, Department of Geography, University of British Columbia. 1970.

[2] Ashcroft Journal, July 22, 1911.

[3] Nelson A. Riis, "Settlement Abandonment — A Case Study of Walhachin."

[4] Ibid.

7 War

Foot drill at Walhachin.

Since the summer of 1911, the Walhachin company of the 31st British Columbia Horse had been holding thrice-weekly drills in the fields which surrounded the town. Each summer thereafter, the more than twenty resident Walhachin members of "C" Company attended the annual summer training camp at Vernon, British Columbia. And in June, 1914, when war broke out in Europe, the Walhachin company prepared for mobilization. Parades and rifle practices went on at an increased pace. Then early in August the 31st British Columbia Horse was ordered to Quebec as part of the First Canadian Expeditionary Force. From there they proceeded almost immediately to England to be stationed at Salisbury Plain with the other Canadian regiments. "C" Company of the 31st British Columbia Horse was under the command of Captain R.E. Paget.

Those other orchardists of military age who had been affiliated with military units in Britain returned immediately to rejoin their regiments. Those who were neither cavalrymen, nor attached to a British Reserve Regiment joined one of the other Canadian regiments.

Within a month of war being declared, forty-three of the English orchardists had left for active service. And in the ensuing months more and more men enlisted until Walhachin was credited with having the highest enlistment rate per capita of any city in Canada. By 1916 no English orchardists of military age remained in the settlement, and only a handful of older ones. The men who remained were either CPR employees (of whom there were a large number) or hired orchard labourers.

Many of the English wives also left Walhachin in August,

1914. They were in such a rush to return home with their husbands that they packed only what they could carry with them. Their furniture, china, valuable pictures and even their personal trinkets were all left behind. Perhaps the prospect of escaping the privations of frontier living which they had endured for four years, and the thought of returning to the comforts of English society were more important to them than their personal possessions. Or perhaps it was just that they, like everyone else, firmly believed the war would be over in a matter of months and that they would soon be back in Walhachin again. Certainly, it is easy to see why that belief was widely held when reports such as these were common in every newspaper:

"London, August 29, 1914: A prominent diplomat of the highest official standing in a neutral government who happens to

Some members of "C" Company, 31st B.C. Horse, as they drilled in the fields beyond the townsite.

be in Europe observing the developments predicts that the Kaiser will make the first overture for peace in two months. He said, 'It is evident that the Russian advance will make the German position untenable in the long run. It is equally evident that the Kaiser cannot afford to let the Fatherland be crushed in the final stage of the struggle, as final defeat even after initial victories would mean the probable loss of his Imperial crown, and serious internal trouble in Germany'.

"Diplomats who first took the view that there would be a fight to the finish are now taking the view that the Kaiser will end the struggle with a grand flourish of German trumpets, even though Germany gets no fruits of victory."[1]

"September 12, 1914: A letter from a high German officer invalided home, seen by a Post correspondent, says: '. . . The

89

war is not going quite as we expected. The resistance of the Allied forces is extraordinary. The German losses are so terrible that the Emperor has forbidden their disclosure. Our generals have been wantonly wasteful with our men, who have been mowed down by the thousands . . .'."[2]

It was no wonder that everyone expected the war to be over by Christmas. But it was not. And as the fighting continued and as men poured into Gallipoli and into the trenches in Belgium and France, more and more men from Walhachin enlisted. And now the struggle began for the handful of older men, women and children who remained in the settlement, to keep the orchards alive. They had to keep the trees pruned and free from pests — to keep ice from forming over the branches in the winter — to keep wooden supports jammed up under the overladen branches at harvest — to pick and pack the apples for shipping — to saw free the branches broken in every severe wind storm, and to seal the tears on the trunks so the trees themselves would not die. And the most difficult job of all was to keep the ramshackle irrigation flume in working condition for repairs were needed constantly. Each spring flash floods washed out a tressle, or broke through a section of trough. Each year with high water in the river, the heavy twelve-inch wooden pipe that had been suspended from the north shore to the south shore had to be carefully watched and cleared of water as soon as it dipped dangerously close to the level of the river. And when this clearing was necessary and the flow of water from the flume had to be discontinued, some areas of the orchard on the south shore which did not receive adequate water from the canal system running out of the creeks had to be hand watered.

But despite everything, the orchards continued to grow and the production of apples continued. In 1915 a crop similar in size to that of 1914 was harvested and sent to market. In 1916 this volume increased. In 1917 and in 1918 records were set as production figures each year exceeded 1,500 boxes of apples. Each box sold for approximately three dollars, and despite high production costs and American competition, things looked promising for the orchards at Walhachin.

A prime concern, of course, for all those who remained in the settlement, in addition to the determination to keep the orchards alive for their men to come back to, was the welfare of the men themselves. There were Walhachin residents in all branches of the service. Regular gifts of cigarettes and tobacco, "home" newspapers and personal letters went from Walhachin to men in Mesopotamia and Belgium by way of a general

Canadian Forces mailing address in London. And a steady flow of letters and Active Service Postcards returned to the orchard settlement. The letters were full of news, but it is hard to imagine the feelings of frustration and disappointment which must have accompanied the receipt of an official Active Service Postcard. It was a formal card containing a list of printed statements, and it was the only communication that was allowed to be sent home from troops stationed on the front line.

It looked like this:

NOTHING is to be written on this side except the date and signature of the sender. Sentences not required may be crossed out.

If anything else is added the postcard will be destroyed.

I am quite well.

I have been admitted into hospital — and am getting on well. and hope to be discharged soon.

I am being sent down to the base.

I have received your —
letter dated . . . . .
telegram dated .   .   .   .   .
parcel dated . . . . . .

Letter follows at first opportunity.

I have received no letter from you —
lately.
for a long time.

Signature . . . .
Date . . . .

Someone who awaited news for weeks or perhaps months could hardly be blamed for feeling cheated on receipt of such a postcard with one single line left showing.

But when men were sent down from the line or were on leave in England, they were allowed to write fairly freely. Some of the letters sent back to Walhachin painted a graphic picture of what life was like in the trenches.

"November, 1915: In June we left the muddy Salisbury Plain and sailed for France. Since then I have had quite an exciting time, believe me. Many a time I thought I would never see daylight and I must thank God that I am alive and well today. The first place we went to when we came to France was Givenchy, near La Basse, where we made an attack on September 25th. After a week there the Canadian Division moved to a new part of the line in Belgium where we spent three months. I must tell you we are at present dismounted and acting the same as Infantry up in the trenches. As you know horses are no use in this war unless we get 'em in the open, and they refuse to do that.

"I was in the front line when the attack was made on Loose. Many a time we just lay in our dug-outs when the shells fell all around and waited on death, for if one of them fell anywhere near you, your number was up. A few days ago we were out on a digging party and ran into an old used French battery, and saw one of the ammunition wagons still up to the axle in mud. And there were shells galore. They'd make good souveniers, but they are too heavy to carry.

"I am sitting now in a pile of straw in an old cowshed. My hands are so cold I can hardly write. This is only November 16th — the winter is only coming in. I do wish it was all over. . . ."

"June, 1915: Many thanks for your letter and cigarettes. They arrived at a critical moment. We were just going to move to the trenches again and none of us had any smokes. Either we all have parcels at once or no one has any at all. And it's much the same with the fighting. It's either 'hell-a-popping' or just as peaceful as sitting on the river bank at Walhachin.

"Your gala May 24th celebrations sound like they were a great success in spite of the rainy weather. Our May 24th was quite different. We were in the reserve trench at Festibert the day before Mr. Tennant was killed, and we were heavily shelled on and off all day. In fact it was quite the most exciting 24th any of us have spent. A man has just gone walking by with his head all bandaged. He had been hit in the eye by a piece of an explosive bullet, which by the way, is supposed to have been banned by international agreement. '

"This country has been occupied by small farmers, so there are plenty of old stables where we sleep. If there is no stable, we sleep on the meadows. We are in reserve just now lying behind a hedge. . . . We still hope to get the horses back some time in the future.[2]

". . . Basil Loyd and I are going to order a box of Walhachin apples to be sent out. The majority of fruit trees here are pear. They're not ripe yet, but they won't last long once they do get ripe. We often talk of Walhachin, and the many pleasant happenings there. . . ."[3]

"July, 1916: From where we are we can ride up to the front lines in about one and a half hours and see everything. Officers are allowed up any time. In fact they are encouraged to go so that we know our way about when we go up for business. There are thousands of guns and they are roaring all the time. The Germans are getting back what they have been giving our men since the war began. Last night while we were having supper a shell burst about half a mile away. We didn't know if it had been fired from a gun or dropped from an airplane.

"The work going on is wonderful. Gangs of men follow up the fighting men, picking up all equipment — ammunition, tools, bombs and so forth. Other parties are busy burying the dead. Others are making roads, filling in trenches or bridging them, while still others are laying telephone wires and water pipes for drinking water. Then the big guns are being shifted, and lorries are following them with ammunition and rations. It's a tremendous affair. The wet weather has made it much more difficult. I guess we all want the war to finish, and it looks to be in the last stage, but how long this stage lasts can't be seen yet."[4]

But despite the high percentage of orchardists who had enlisted in the armed forces, and despite the problems facing the few who had remained of maintaining the orchards and keeping the irrigation system working, it is not true that the outbreak of war and the departure of so many men was primarily responsible for the failure of the orchard project. Certainly, the job of keeping the orchards alive was difficult. During those four years of war, each of the older orchardists who had remained behind had six or more ten-acre holdings to care for all by himself. As a result, he could not give the trees the careful pruning, spraying and care they required.

It is also true that there were periods during those years when the irrigation system was temporarily inoperable. Each spring, flash floods occurred and created damage which took weeks for the few remaining men to repair.

But the orchards survived all this. They even survived what could have been the most serious calamity of all. In April, 1918, the most severe storm the orchard settlement had ever experienced struck without warning. Two days of driving rain accompanied by gale force winds uprooted many trees and tore hundreds of branches off others. But more important, the storm

washed out the shallow foundations of a whole row of wooden tressles. And because of the orchardists' failure to build the trough in separate sections, more than one-quarter mile of flume was twisted down. The damage occurred on one of the steepest sections of the hillside. If there had been sufficient manpower to make the repairs, this huge break might have been spanned in time to provide water to the apple trees for at least the final few weeks of summer, but with so few men left, repairs were not even attempted. The trees were left to suffer through an entire growing season without irrigation of any kind. And they even survived that.

Finally the war ended, but then the orchard project received another blow. Many of the men from Walhachin who had survived, discovered that they could find good-paying jobs back

The women worked beside the few remaining men sorting apples in the community hall.

in England, and decided not to return to the orchard settlement after all. Others, who had returned to England at their own expense to rejoin British regiments, were reluctant to pay their own transportation back to Canada, particularly with the knowledge of the damage that had been done to the flume and the amount of work and money that would be necessary to put the orchards back into top shape. And so, they too elected not to return.

But in spite of everything, there were others who were anxious to return, and even the knowledge of the damage to the irrigation system did nothing to deter them. Some brought back the wives who had departed so precipitately in 1914 and others brought new war brides. Included in the lists of those who returned were Frank Ivatt, "Rafe" Chetwynd, E.J.V. Askew,

John Tuerning, A.R. Willan, E. Flowerdew, (Gordon's brother) E.J.B. Kitson, Tom Edwards and Eric Ferguson. But their numbers were sadly depleted, and the total population of the settlement was far below the 150 that it had boasted on the eve of the outbreak of war.

And now, unfortunately those men who returned discovered that what had been reported to them in letters as having been "considerable damage" to the flume, was in fact almost irreparable. At least it was irreparable without considerable financial outlay which the depleted number of orchardists could not underwrite. Once again the assistance of a financial backer was required. But the man who had taken over the interests of the BCDA during the seven years since 1912 when the London-based company had withdrawn its support from the orchard project, was himself in financial difficulties. When the Marquis of Angelsey had inherited the title from his cousin, Henry Cyril Paget, he had also inherited the fifth Earl's debts which were reported to be in excess of $500,000. In addition, "On his last visit to Walhachin before the war, the Marquis had invested heavily in one of the five hundred oil companies that had been formed in Calgary as a result of the Turner Valley Oil boom. Unfortunately, the company he invested in had never advanced beyond the paper stage. All the money he had invested was lost. He had been forced to sell his family estate in Staffordshire to provide himself with sufficient capital to carry on with his own affairs."[5]

Accordingly, it is not surprising that when he was approached by the orchardists at Walhachin in 1919 to provide money for the rebuilding of the irrigation system and for the replanting of a considerable area of damaged trees, he was forced to refuse. But, he did not wish to see the orchard project die. And since its only chance for survival lay in the rebuilding of the irrigation system, the Marquis agreed to approach the government of British Columbia on behalf of the orchardists.

Some time earlier the British Columbia government had stated publicly that it intended to establish a number of government-sponsored land settlement schemes for returning soldiers. Accordingly, the Marquis approached the government and offered his entire Walhachin property — all 5,000 acres — as a gift to be used for this purpose.

Both the Marquis and the orchardists anticipated an enthusiastic acceptance of this offer. The Walhachin project had been watched with sympathetic interest and given enthusiastic encouragement ever since its inception. British Columbia's Premier Sir Richard McBride had boasted of the potential of his province as a fruit growing area not only to cities across Canada, but also in Britain and the United States. He had been instrumental in the organization of a Canadian Fruit Growers' Convention and he was directly responsible for that convention holding its meetings in Vancouver. He had also been responsible for the establishment of five experimental orchards — three in the Okanagan and two in the central Interior — and he had repeatedly sponsored trips around the province by agriculturalists, promoting better farming methods for orchardists and discussing such pertinent matters as correct packing methods, proper pruning and better preventative measures against frost damage.

But unfortunately the province had undergone a change of political leadership. Sir Richard McBride, himself an upper-class Englishman and the leader of the pro-British provincial Conservative party, had been replaced by John Oliver and the Liberals. According to historian Margaret Ormsby, Oliver was the direct antithesis of McBride — a man of little formal education and the son of lower-class parents.[6] When the Marquis, on behalf of the Walhachin orchardists, suggested that the government take over the Walhachin property for use as a settlement area for returning servicemen and finance the rebuilding of the irrigation system so the land could continue to be used as an orchard area, Oliver refused, seemingly for no other reason than because of a personal dislike for upper-class Englishmen. Instead of accepting the gift of 5,000 acres of property at Walhachin for a soldiers' settlement area, Premier John Oliver elected to buy a piece of property from the South Okanagan Land Company. Perhaps the piece of land he had purchased was more suited to agricultural development than were the benchlands of the Thompson, but to the orchardists at Walhachin his decision seemed unjustified.

It was also unfortunate, for it meant the end of the orchard community. A study was done before the land was offered to Oliver for his soldiers' settlement area, to determine exactly how much money would be necessary to put the irrigation system into proper working order. The result of that study had been that the repair and upgrading of the flume and ditches in order to construct what was termed an acceptable irrigation system, would require an estimated outlay of approximately $240,000. It was impossible for the orchardists to raise such a sum themselves. Without government assistance it was impossible for them to continue to try to keep the orchards at Walhachin alive. And once again families began to leave the settlement, either to return to England or to seek positions in other Canadian centers. It is perhaps ironical that this final exodus should have occurred just when the English community had begun to shake itself free of that class distinction which so many of the residents themselves had deplored, and which had marred the relationship between Walhachin and the surrounding centers. Without doubt, four years of war had done much to soften this class consciousness. Certainly, the fact that only a small number of the actually "titled" members of the original group had returned had a great deal to do with it. In these months after the end of the war there were new feelings of equality and mutual respect among all members of the orchard community which had been noticeably lacking. But unfortunately this lowering of class lines and this increase in understanding, which might have done much to save the whole project if it occurred nine years earlier, came too late to make any difference. It was obvious that the orchard settlement was finished. Once again, by two's and three's the men and women of Walhachin packed up and left. And this time those possessions which they did not bother to pack up and take with them were not carefully kept in storage awaiting their eventual return. Following the hurried departure of the orchardists in 1914, the heavy furniture, dishes, linens and pictures had been carefully stored until the war ended. But this time everything which was unclaimed was offered for auction.

The families of CPR personnel, who now comprised the bulk of the citizenry of Walhachin, picked up treasured heirlooms at a fraction of their value — a wooden four-poster bed with hand-carved roses on the four corner posts — a solid mahogany butler's tray with tiny legs hidden in the carrying handles which could be let down so the tray could be set on the floor beside the hostess as she served afternoon tea or evening refreshments — English bone china — sterling silver tea services — even personal articles of clothing.

By the end of the summer of 1921 the last futile attempts to keep the flume functioning, even to a limited degree, were discontinued. The irrigation system ceased to operate in any capacity, and by 1922 the last of the English settlers moved away. Among the last to leave was Rafe Chetwynd, manager since 1919. His position was then filled by a man named Johnston, but Johnston was hired with specific instructions not to undertake any plans for rebuilding the settlement, but to dispose of the property as quickly as possible.

However, this disposal of the property was not accomplished until nearly two decades later. In 1940, Harry

Ferguson, a Canadian cattleman, leased the Walhachin property from the Marquis with the intention of using it as grazing land. In 1947, he bought it outright for the sum of $40,000.[7] This included the entire 5,000 acres with the exception of the twelve acres which held the Walhachin townsite and three other lots on which families in England had continued to pay taxes ever since 1910. Ferguson wanted the property for use as winter grazing range, and so the orchard fields were allowed to return to their natural grassland state.

Twenty years later a new attempt was made to put the benchlands of the Thompson to increased agricultural use. This time it was decided to use the fields of Walhachin for the development of a strain of charolais cattle, but the land could not support the density of livestock that were set to feed upon it, and this experiment, too was later abandoned.

In 1953, the British Columbia Department of Agriculture undertook a study of the land at Walhachin.[8] That study revealed that of the 5,000 acres which the orchardists had purchased, not one acre was considered to be suitable for fruit production and only 160 acres — less than three per cent of the total — were suitable for vegetable production. A further study of the soil conditions at Walhachin was undertaken in 1962.[9] As a result of that study, the Provincial Department of Agriculture issued a statement which said that the land at Walhachin was suited for nothing but use as casual grazing land — the use to which Pennie and Greaves had put it in the years leading up to 1909.

Footnotes:

[1] Ashcroft Journal, August 29, 1914.

[2] Ashcroft Journal, September 12, 1914.

[3] Personal letter from Lieutenant Gordon Flowerdew to Miss Isa Bennie.

[4] Ibid.

[5] Nelson A. Riis, "Settlement Abandonment — A Case Study of Walhachin." Unpublished Master's Thesis, Department of Geography, University of British Columbia, 1970.

[6] Margaret A. Ormsby, *British Columbia: A History.* Macmillan of Canada, Toronto, 1958.

[7] Nelson A. Riis, "Settlement Abandonment — A Case Study of Walhachin."

[8] Ibid.

Catastrophe or Camelot?

And so, the orchard settlement at Walhachin was finished. A major contributing cause was the complete lack of information which existed in the minds of the orchardists and of the promoters of the project concerning the enterprise on which they were embarking, and the area in which this enterprise was to be established.

Another factor which played a part in the failure was the fact that the orchardists were dealing with a product which took four to six years to mature. Had they been growing berry fruits or grain, weather damage to a crop would have resulted in the loss of a single year's profits, but for the orchardists, a bad year which actually destroyed some of the trees meant a loss of profit in that area for anywhere from four to six years.

Of course, the mistakes made in the construction of the flume and in the irrigation ditches were critical, but even if the irrigation system had been constructed so that huge sections would not twist down each time there was a minor washout — so that forty per cent of the water coming down the flume would not be lost to seepage in the unlined ditches — so that the tressles would not be unsteady on their shallow footings — even if the irrigation system had worked properly, the orchard project at Walhachin would still have failed. For the amount of arable acreage available simply could not support the expense of constructing and maintaining the irrigation system or the number of orchardists involved in the project. Nor could anything be done about the inescapable paradox — the personality of the orchardists themselves.

The apple trees continue to bloom despite the dry and rocky soil of Walhachin.

And so the dream was over, but the memory remains: A handful of Englishmen set out to grow fruit trees in the desert and to create for themselves a leisured, cultured lifestyle in the Canadian wilderness. And they succeeded. For nine years Walhachin, like King Arthur's Camelot, had its "moment." "Brief," certainly, but none the less "shining."

101

RESIDENTS OF WALHACHIN IN 1914

J. S. W. Anderson
Mr. and Mrs. E. J. V. Askew
C. S. Bainbridge
Mr. and Mrs. Charles E. Barnes
Mrs. A. C. Baxter and
    two young sons
R. S. M. Beatson
Mrs. Bell
Mrs. John Bennie, Miss Isa
    Bennie and Master Andrew
Mr. Benning
Mr. and Mrs. J. Bertram
    and infant son
Mr. Biden
Mr. and Mrs. E. E. Billinghurst
L. Blair
Mr. Brown
G. Calder
Mr. and Mrs. Clifford Campbell
J. Carlendar
Captain Carlyon
Ralph Chetwynd
Mrs. Chetwynd (mother)
A. H. T. Chetwynd (cousin)
Sir Edward Chirchester, Bart.
J. C. Clarke
C. H. Cockburn
Mr. and Mrs. C. Collingwood
Miss Collingwood, C.M.E.
R. J. Colson
Mr. and Mrs. Cooks
J. W. Crawford

R. O. Crewe-Reid
K. G. DeJeagh
Colonel Dennys
Mr. and Mrs. B. F. Durant
A. E. East
Mrs. Grey Edwards
Thomas Edwards
F. Falvey-Beyts
C. A. Fellows
Cecil Fielder
Audrey Flowerdew
Eleanor Flowerdew
Gordon Flowerdew
E. Flowerdew
Mr. and Mrs. B. C. Footner
    and son Vernon
W. A. Fortescue
Mr. Fuller
Miss Gandy
C. T. Gardner
Mr. and Mrs. George
Miss George
V. Goggin
N. E. Gore-Langton
A. L. Green
Frank Groome
M. A. Gruen
James Haddock
R. Halliday
Mr. and Mrs. Hamilton-Warde
Captain Harrison
M. W. Hemming

W. Miller Higgs
Walter B. Hill
T. E. Hollerton
Mr. and Mrs. J. P. Hunt
Mr. and Mrs. Frank Ivatt
Miss Ivatt
W. A. Jefferies
Miss Freda Kendall
A. Kinch
Mr. Kingdon
E. J. B. Kitson
W. P. Knatchbull
Mr. Knight
W. Langley
A. K. Loyd   Lloyd
B. Loyd   LLoyd
E. P. Lloyd
Colin Mackenzie-Kennedy
Mr. Marshall
E. E. Mann
J. Martin
J. L. Melkuish
F. Mieville
L. N. Moxley
A. Munro
Hon. H. M. and Mrs.
    Nelson-Hood
Mr. Ord
L. G. Paget
R. E. Paget (Captain C
    Company 31st B.C. Horse)
Jervis Parker

B. Parkin
V. C. Pearce
Captain and Mrs. Herbert
    Peebles
H. L. Penkeith
J. Pike
Reginald Pole
A. P. Prior
H. J. Pugh
G. E. Ratcliffe
Mr. Redmayne
Mr. Rhodes
Miss Rice
Miss Netta Ricketts
R. Roberts
W. Rodolph
E. S. Salaman
Miss Josie Scott-Elliott
W. T. Shore
W. H. Snell
C. T. Soames
R. T. Sparkles
Mr. Stuart-McLaren
W. S. Tennant
H. Tripp
John Tuering
R. Turner
Miss I. N. Twining
R. A. Wallace
J. Wallington
Mr. and Mr. E. R. Wilkenson
A. R. Willan
Miss Ruth Wortley-Watson

INDEX